VIC 20
EXPOSED

First Published in the United Kingdom by
Melbourne House (Publishers) Ltd.

This Remastered Edition
Published by
Acorn Books
www.acornbooks.co.uk

This book was edited by John Vander Reyden.
Authors that contributed include:
      Dr. Ian Logan
      Lee De Forest
      Peter Falconer

VIC 20 EXPOSED

EDITED BY

JOHN VANDER REYDEN

MELBOURNE HOUSE

Contents

Appendices

CHAPTER 1

PROGRAMMING IN BASIC

BASIC is only one of the many languages used to communicate with computers. It is however, the most common language in the microcomputer world, so it's a good one to know. BASIC varies from computer to computer, but once one dialect is known it is easy to adapt to others. A knowledge of VIC 20 BASIC is a solid basis for programming in BASIC on any computer.

VIC 20 BASIC

Immediate and Program modes.

When the VIC 20 is turned on it starts in immediate mode. In this mode, each line typed in and completed by pressing RETURN is executed immediately – hence the name.

Program mode is used to store programs. The name is something of a misnomer, but it is commonly used. Actually, you're still in immediate mode, but whenever BASIC sees a line that starts with a number, it executes the line by storing it in memory. The statements following the line number are executed only when you run the program.

e.g.   typing   PRINT "HELLO" will cause HELLO to be displayed on the screen.

typing   10 PRINT "HELLO" will cause that line to be stored in memory. There will be no display until you type RUN.

Points to note:

- Line numbers must be integers from 0 to 63999.
- Lines are sorted into numerical order no matter in what order they're typed.
- Typing a line number, then pressing RETURN deletes that line.
- Typing two lines with the same line number leaves only the second line in the program.
- Typing NEW deletes all program lines in memory so that you can type in a new program. If you don't do this the new program may have lines from the old program in it.
- To BASIC, a line can be up to 88 characters long (including the RETURN to terminate it) – ie. 4 screen rows. If you continue typing after this, none of the line will be stored in the program (if in program mode) or executed (if in immediate mode).
- You may put more than one statement on a line by seperating them with a colon.

e.g.   PRINT "H" : PRINT "E" : PRINT "L" : PRINT "L" : PRINT "O"

This can be done in both program and immediate modes.

- It is a good idea to start numbering lines at 100, and increasing at intervals of 10 or 20. This enables you to insert lines between existing lines.
- Although the BASIC interpreter stores any spaces you put in program lines, it ignores them when it executes. All spaces may therefore be omitted, although this makes programs difficult to read. The spaces are stored and when you list the program they are included in the listing. You cannot insert any spaces into keywords.

Control Structures

These are statements which control the order in which program lines are executed. BASIC has the simplest control structure — sequential execution — built in. In the absence of any other control structure, a program is executed from the lowest to the highest numbered line. If this were the only control structure available, programs would be very limited, so VIC 20 BASIC has the following statements for program control. They allow your programs to make decisions, perform loops, and branch to different parts of the program.

IF — THEN

IF [expression] THEN [statement(s)]
e.g.   10 IF A=5 THEN B=A−1 : GOTO 200
        20 IF (A < 0 AND A > −3) THEN GOSUB 6000

If the expression is true then all statements following the THEN are executed. In line 10 above, for example, if A=5 then both statements B=A−1 and GOTO 200 are executed. If the expression is false, both statements are ignored, and the next line is executed.

The expression may be arithmetic, in which case the THEN statements are executed if the expression evaluates to any number other than 0. In other words, the VIC20 takes 0 to be FALSE and all else to be TRUE. This isn't particularly useful, and is bad programming style, since it isn't immediately obvious what is meant.

e.g.   IF 5+6 THEN PRINT "YES"
            result — prints YES
        IF A−5 THEN PRINT "YES"
            result — doesn't print if A=5

If the expression evaluates to a string the result is unpredictable.

FOR — NEXT

FOR [variable] = [start] TO [limit] STEP [step]
[statement(s)]
NEXT [variable]

e.g.

10 FOR J=62 TO 70 STEP 1
20 PRINT CHR$ (J) ; "IS ASCII" ; J
30 NEXT J

2

This loops through lines 10-30 in the following way.

(i) J is set to the start value − 62

(ii) statements are executed until a NEXT statement appears

(iii) the STEP factor is added to J. J = 63

(iv) J is compared to the limit value - 70. If J is greater than 70 the loop is finished and execution proceeds from the line following the NEXT statement. If J is less than or equal to 70 the program loops back to line 20. If line 10 had been FOR J=70 TO 62 STEP − 1 the values of J would be decremented by 1 every pass through the loop. When J is compared to the limit value 62 execution of the loop continues if J is greater than or equal to the limit value. Execution does not proceed to the line following the next statement until J is less than 62.

• The FOR variable must be a floating point variable

• [start], [limit] and [step] may be numeric variable names, expressions, negative, positive, integer or floating point.

• "STEP [step]" may be left out, in which case a STEP value of 1 is assumed. So in the example above "STEP 1" is not necessary.

• The variable name in the NEXT statement may be left out. In the example above, line 30 may read "30 NEXT"

• FOR loops are always executed at least once, even if the start value is initially greater than the limit for positive steps or less than the limit value for negative steps. This is because the comparison of the FOR variable with the limit is done at the end of the loop.

• If the step value is negative, the loop is terminated when the FOR variable is less than the limit. Again, the loop will be executed at least once.

• FOR statements may be nested to a maximum depth of 10. That is, you may have loops within loops.

e.g.

```
10 FOR J=1 TO 5
20 FOR K=1 TO 7
30 ...
40 FOR L=1 TO 3
50 ...
60 ...
70 NEXT L
80 NEXT K
90 NEXT J
```

When nesting loops be careful to terminate them correctly. The last FOR variable mentioned must be the first NEXT variable mentioned. If the variable names are left out of the NEXT statments, BASIC terminates the loops correctly. Each loop variable is placed on a stack. The NEXT statement takes the variable from the top. This is always the last one placed there. Hence the computer's "ability" to select the correct NEXT variable.

- There may be more than one variable name in a NEXT statement. The example above could have been terminated by 70 NEXT L,K,J. If you leave the variable names out BASIC will only terminate the last loop for you – ie. "70 NEXT" is only equivalent to "70 NEXT L".

GOTO

GOTO [line–number]
This is the simplest of the control statments. When executed, it causes the program to continue from the line number named. The unrestrained use of GOTOs can make programs difficult to follow, so it should be used with care.
- The line number must exist in the program.
- It cannot be a variable name or an arithmetic expression.

e.g.   10 X=50
       20 GOTO X – incorrect
       20 GOTO (40+30) –incorrect
       20 GOTO 200 – correct if line 200 exists

GOSUB

GOSUB [line–number] / RETURN
GOSUB is short for GO to SUBroutine. A subroutine is a collection of statements terminated by a RETURN statement.
When a GOSUB is executed, the program continues from the line number named, just like a GOTO. But, when the next RETURN statement is reached, the program returns to wherever the GOSUB is, continuing execution from the statement following the GOSUB.

e.g.   10   . . . .
       20   GOSUB 500 ⟶ 500   . . . .
       30   . . . . ↖ 510   . . . .
       40   . . . . ↘ 520   RETURN

The arrows indicate the path the program follows.
Subroutines are useful when there is a task which must be executed several times in the program. Using subroutines means you needn't write the same lines several times – you just GOSUB to them each time you need them.
- A RETURN statement without a GOSUB causes an error
- A RETURN statement is not written by pressing the RETURN key! They are quite different.
- There may be multiple RETURN statements in a subroutine.

e.g.   10 GOSUB 500

       ...
       500 IF X=5 THEN RETURN
       510 IF X=6 THEN B=X : RETURN
       520 C=X
       530 RETURN

This saves you having to jump to the end of the subroutine to a single RETURN

4

- Subroutines may be nested.

e.g. 10 GOSUB 520

     ...

    520 ...
    530 GOSUB 600
    540 ...
    550 RETURN

    ...

    600 ...
    610 GOSUB 700
    620 ...
    630 RETURN

BASIC does this by "stacking" the return addresses. When a GOSUB is reached, its address is put on a stack. At the next GOSUB its address is put on top of the first, and so on. When a RETURN is reached, the address on top of the stack is taken off, and the program branches to that address. At the next RETURN the address next on the stack is taken off, and so on. The addresses are stored in a special area called "stack", which is a fixed size (256 bytes). Therefore, by nesting too many GOSUBs you can run out of stack space. This will cause an "OUT OF MEMORY" error message to be displayed.

ON GOTO/GOSUB

    ON [variable] GOTO [line−number 1] , [line−number 2] ,...
    ON [variable] GOSUB [line−number 1] , [line−number 2] ,...

Depending on the value of the variable, the program will GOTO (or GOSUB) one of the line numbers. If the variable equals 1, the program will GOTO the first line number, if the variable equals 2, it will GOTO the second line number, and so on.

e.g. ON X GOTO 200 , 60 , 60 , 75 , 500

- If the variable is 0 or greater than the number of line-numbers, the statement is ignored, and execution continues from the statement following the ON statement. If the variable is negative, it causes an error.
- The variable may also be an arithmetic expression.

e.g. ON (A * 3 + 4) GOSUB 100 , 1200 , 60
      ON (X−3*Y) GOTO 60 , 60 , 70 , 80 , 900

END

This statements stops the execution of a program. There may be several END statements in a program. This is handy for debugging (ie. getting rid of errors), since after an END has stopped the program, you may check the value of variables (by typing PRINT [variable]), change the value of variables, or look at the program listing (by typing LIST). You may then continue the program by typing CONT. However, CONT won't work if the program stopped on an error, or if you attempt to edit the program.

- It is not necessary to finish a program with an END statement.

DATA STRUCTURES

For a program to be useful it must be able to store information. It does this by using data structures. The following is a brief summary of the data structures available on the VIC 20.

Bits and Bytes

A bit is the basic data structure used in all digital computers. The name is derived from Binary digIT, because a bit can take one of only two values, 1 or 0. Since it would be extremely cumbersome to store information bit by bit, there are more sophisticated data structures available to the programmer.

A byte is 8 bits. It can represent any number from 0 to 255 using the binary number system. The VIC 20 is a byte addressable machine, which means that a byte is the smallest data structure which the programmer can directly examine or change – using PEEK and POKE.

(For more on bits, bytes and the binary number system see the section on Operators.)

Characters

Characters are stored as a code number in 1 byte. Thus there are potentially 256 character codes. The most common code is ASCII (for American Standard Code for Information Interchange). The VIC 20 however, uses a slightly different code so as to cover colours and other special characters. Appendix A contains a table of ASCII and VIC 20 character codes. You may also use CHR$ and ASC to explore VIC 20 character codes.

e.g.   PRINT CHR$ (65) will print the character wth code 65 – an "A"
       PRINT ASC ("B") will print the code for "B" – 66

• There is a difference between numeric characters and numbers. A number is read as a character when it appears between double quotes

e.g.   "5" – the character 5
       5 – the number 5

PRINT ASC ("5") will display the code for the character 5
PRINT ASC (5) won't work.

Variables

In general, when you store information you don't want to:
— decide where in memory to put it
— POKE it byte by byte into memory
— remember where you put it so you can retrieve it.

BASIC provides variables to do this for you. All you have to do is provide a name for your information. BASIC then attends to storage and retrieval of that information.

Rules for naming variables.

1)   The first character must be a letter : A–Z, a–z
2)   Except for the last character, the rest must be letters or numbers.

3) The last character must be —
    — "$" if you're storing strings
    — "%" if you're storing integers
    — a letter or a number if you're storing floating point numbers
e.g. AB$, NAME$ — string variables
      KI%, SKILL% — integer variables
      E2, TEMP — floating point variables
- Variable names can be up to 86 characters long
- However, BASIC only recognises the first two characters plus the last one, if it's either "%" or "$".
e.g. NAME$ is seen as NA$
      NATURE$ is also seen as NA$
      TEMP is seen as TE
      SKILL% is seen as SK%
So don't use names like TEMP1 and TEMP2, since BASIC will treat them as one variable. Make sure different variable names differ in the first or second character.
- The advantage of long variable names is that they make programs easier to understand.
The disadvantage is that they take up more memory.
- Different variable types can have what appears to be the same name.
e.g. NA$, NA% and NA are all different variables.
- Variable names must not contain reserved words — ie. words which BASIC recognises as commands.
e.g. BASIC would read TOP$ as TO P$ since TO is a reserved word. This is a consequence of spaces between keywords and variables being optional.
FIRSTHENS would be read as FIRS THEN S since THEN is a reserved word.
This type of thing usually results in a SYNTAX ERROR in lines that look OK.
- Assigning values to variables is done using "="
e.g. NAME$ =   "JOHN"
      SKILL% =   50
      FROD$ =   NAME$ — this assigns the value of
                                  NAME$ to FROD$

      SKILL% =   SKILL% + 10   — this takes the old value of
                                  SKILL%, adds 10, and assigns
                                  the result as the new value of
                                  SKILL%
- As the name implies, the value of variables may vary.
- Only the correct type of information may be assigned to a variable. Trying to assign a number to a string variable, or a string to a numeric variable will cause a TYPE MISMATCH error.
e.g. NAME$ = 72 — type mismatch
      SKILL% = "HARRY" — type mismatch

String Variables

A string is a series of characters contained within opening and closing quotes.

e.g. "This is a string"

Thisisnotastringitisaverylongvariablename

• Strings can be concatenated – ie. joined together using the "+" symbol

e.g. B$ = "THE VIC "

A$ = B$ + "20"

The value of A$ is now the string "THE VIC 20"

• Concatenation can be used to put character in strings that you couldn't normally put in – for example, the double quote character.

e.g. A$ = " "STRING" " will not work because it will be read as an empty string (" "), then STRING, then another empty string. This will not make sense to BASIC

A$ = CHR$ (34) + "STRING" + CHR$ (34)

This concatenates the value of CHR$ (34), ", with STRING and " giving "STRING"

This technique can also be used to give multicoloured displays

e.g. A$ = CHR$ (30) +"THE" + CHR$ (31) + "END"

PRINT A$ will now display a green THE and a blue END.

• String variables can be very useful in getting "bombproof" input from the keyboard.

For example, imagine you are writing a program which at some point prompts the user to type in a number. You can do this by using

INPUT "NUMBER",A

To execute this the VIC 20 prints the string and a question mark, and waits for the user to type in a number which it will assign as the value of A. But, if the user types in a non-numeric character, this will cause the error message REDO FROM START to be displayed. It skips down a line and displays the question mark again, waiting for a number. It will continue to do this until a number is input, or the program is stopped. This can be confusing to a user who doesn't know the meaning of REDO FROM START, and it can also destroy screen displays.

To avoid this, use

INPUT "NUMBER",A$

Now the VIC 20 expects a string, so whatever(almost) the user types will be OK. Of course this means that the program will have to do a little more work, converting the string to a number. To do this, use

A=VAL(A$)

If A$ is a string containing only a number, A will become that number

e.g. A$ = "7.63"

A = VAL (A$)

The value of A is now 7.63

If A$ contains non-numeric characters, VAL(A$) will return 0. Thus, the programmer can arrange to print meaningful error messages and

8

reprompt the user without destroying screen displays.
- VIC 20 BASIC has extensive string manipulation functions – RIGHT$, LEFT$, MID$, + (see VIC 20 BASIC Commands)
- If no value is given to a string variable, its value is the empty string.

Floating Point Variables

Floating point numbers can be integers, fractions preceded by a decimal point, or a combination of the two.

e.g. 6, 7.346, 0.593, -0.762, -3
- They can be up to 9 digits long
- If a number with 10 or more digits is entered, it is automatically converted to scientific notation.

e.g. 12345678912
is displayed as -
1.23456789E+10

The number after the E indicates the number of positions the decimal point must be moved to give its true position. If it is positive, the decimal point is shifted to the right; if negative, to the left.

Note that the last two digits in the original number are rounded off. In general, if the 10th digit is 5 or more, the number is rounded up. If it is 4 or less, it is rounded down.

e.g. 1234567886 is displayed as 1.23456789E+9
.1000000014 is displayed as .100000001
- There is a limit to the size of the numbers the VIC 20 can handle
smallest > 2.93873588E$-$39
largest < 1.70141183E+38

Any number smaller than the lower limit is treated as 0. Any number larger than the upper limit gives an OVERFLOW ERROR.
- Floating point numbers can be entered from the keyboard in scientific notation.
- Floating point variables don't have a special last character
e.g. FP, FLOAT, X, L1
- If no value is given to a floating point variable, its value is 0

Integer Variables

Integers are numbers without a decimal point. They may be negative or positive. Unsigned integers are assumed to be positive.

e.g. 6, +63, -7, -7934621
- Integer variables are distinguished by % as the last character.
e.g. NUM%, SC%, F%
- Integers may be assigned to floating point variables since they are a subset of floating point numbers. However, they will take 5 bytes for storage compared to 2 bytes if assigned to integer variables.
- If no value is given to an integer variable its value is 0.
- In most calculations the VIC 20 converts integers to floating point numbers and, if necessary, converts the result back to an integer. It is

therefore slower to use integer variables than to use floating point variables.

Arrays

Arrays are used to store large amounts of related information without having to assign a variable name to each data item. Instead, a name is assigned to the array as a whole, and the individual data items are referred to by their position in the array.
* Arrays are set up using a DIM statement
e.g. DIM A$ (12)
This will set up a 1 dimensional string array with 13 elements. There are 13 because numbering of array elements starts from 0. This array has the elements A$ (0) through to A$ (12).
    DIM B% (4)
This sets up an integer array of 5 elements − B% (0) to B% (4)
    DIM C (2,4)
This sets up a 2 dimensional floating point array with 15 elements, 3 rows each of 5 elements.

C (0,0)	C (0,1)	C (0,2)	C (0,3)	C (0,4)
C (1,0)	C (1,1)	C (1,2)	C (1,3)	C (1,4)
C (2,0)	C (2,1)	C (2,2)	C (2,3)	C (2,4)

    DIM D$ (1,1,1)
This sets up a 3 dimensional string array of 8 elements − D$ (0,0,0) to D$ (1,1,1)
* Array elements are used just as a variable of the same type is.
e.g. PRINT C (1.3)
    X=C (2,1)
    D$ (1,0,1)="HI"
* You cannot refer to the entire array at one time.
e.g. "PRINT A$" will not display the 13 elements of the array A$. To do this you would need the following:
    FOR J=0 TO 12 : PRINT A$ (J) : NEXT
* Arrays can hold only one type of data. An attempt to store an integer in a string array, or a string in a floating point array will produce a TYPE MISMATCH error.
* Like varables, array elements have default values. When an array is first DIMensioned, all its elements take the default value for that variable type. ie. a string array is filled with null strings, a numeric array is filled with 0's.
* Arrays can also have default sizes. That is, you can refer to an array element without having first DIMensioned the array. However, this only applies to 1 dimensional arrays. The default DIMension is 10 − ie. 11 elements. In this case the VIC 20 has implicitly DIMensioned the array for you. This can be confusing when the program is read later, so it's better to explicitly DIMension all arrays − ie. use a DIM statement.

- Arrays can be DIMensioned only once in a program. This also applies to arrays the VIC 20 has implicitly DIMensioned for you. In other words,

      10 LET A (1) = 0
      20 DIM A (5)
will result in a RE−DIMENSIONED ARRAY error

Operators

Expressions are made up of operators and operands. Operators are symbols recognized by the VIC 20 as representing operations to be performed on the operands. Operands may be variables, constants or other expressions. Expressions return a value, and hence may be used almost anywhere a variable of the same type could be used. There are exceptions to this however, such as GOTO statements. These exceptions are explicitly noted in the description of BASIC commands.

Arithmetic Operators

Arithmetic expressions return an integer value if all operands are integers, and a floating point value if any of the operands are floating point numbers. Most of these operators you will have met before, so a few examples will suffice.

Addition '+'
6+4, B%+C+6

Subtraction '−'
7−3, 18−36, B%−C
The minus sign is also used to signify a negative number.

Multiplication '*'
7*3, B%*8, 16*C*B%

Division '/'
The value on the left of the slash is divided by the value on the right.
7/4, B%/C

Exponentiation ' ↑ '
The value on the left of the arrow is raised to the power of the value on the right.
A ↑ 5, 2 ↑ 3, 6 ↑ B%

Order of evaluation
An expression may contain multiple operators. The order of evaluation of the sub-expressions depends on the precedence of the operator in each sub-expression. Operators with the highest precedence are carried out first. A table of operator precedences appears at the end of the section on operators.

String Operators

Concatenation '+'
The plus sign can also be used to concatenate strings.

e.g. "FREE" + "DOM" returns "FREEDOM"
     if A$="STING" and B$="RAY"
     A$+B$ returns "STINGRAY"

Concatenation can be used to build strings up to 255 characters long. An attempt to build a longer string will result in a STRING TOO LONG error.

Relational Operators

These are used to compare strings or numbers. If the expression is true, −1 is returned, if false, 0 is returned. This means that it is possible to perform arithmetic operations on the result of a relational expression. The operators are:

'='	:	equals
' >	:	is greater than
' <	:	is less than
'= < ' or ' < ='	:	is less than or equal to
'= > or ' > ='	:	is greater than or equal to
' < > '	:	not equal to

e.g. 6 = 6 - returns true (−1)
      6 < 4 - returns false (0)
      6 < 6 - returns 0
      6 < = 6 - returns −1
      A% < > B% - result depends on the value of A%, B%

Strings can calso be compared. This is done character by character, using the VIC 20 character code.

e.g. "C" < "D" returns true (−1) since the code for 'C'−67− is less than the code for 'D'−68
      "CAT" > "CATION" results in false (0)
      A$=C$+D$ result depends on the values of A$, C$ and D$

Boolean Operators

These, named after the logician George Boole, are used to carry out logical operations.

AND

The result of an AND expression is true only if both operands are true, false otherwise.

e.g. 6 > 5 AND 4 < 5 returns true
      6 < 5 AND 4 < 5 returns false
      6 > 5 AND 5 < 4 returns false

IF A=22 AND B=20 GOTO 600 − result: GOTO line 600 if both A=22 and B=20

OR

The result of an OR expression is true if either operand is true, false only if both operands are false.

e.g. 6 > 5 OR 4 < 5 returns true
      6 < 5 OR 4 < 5 returns true
      6 < 5 OR 5 < 4 returns false

IF A=22 OR B=20 OR C=6 THEN GOSUB 20 – result: GOSUB 20 if any of the conditions are true

NOT

This takes only one operand. The result is the logical opposite of the operand.

e.g. NOT (6 > 5) returns false

NOT (6 < 5 OR 4 < 5) returns false

A single operand can be tested for true or false. It acts as if it has ' < > 0' appearing after it, so any value other than 0 will return true.

e.g. IF 6 THEN GOTO 60 – result: GOTO executed

IF AHIT% THEN GOSUB 700 - result: depends on the value of the variable AHIT%

Boolean operations can also be carried out on bits. However, this is best described after a more detailed discussion of the binary number system.

Table of Operator Precedences

Precedence	Operator	Meaning
9	()	used to over-ride normal precedences
8	↑	exponentiation
7	—	signifies negative number
6	*	multiplication
6	/	division
5	+	addition, concuteration
5	—	subtraction
4	=	equals
4	< >	not equal to
4	<	less than
4	>	greater than
4	< = or = <	less than or equal to
4	> = or = >	greater than or equal to
3	NOT	logical opposite
2	AND	logical AND
1	OR	logical inclusive OR

• As noted above, parentheses, (), can be used to over–ride precedences. You can, for example, force an addition to be carried out before a multiplication by parenthesising the addition expression.

e.g. 4*6+2 returns 26

4* (6+2) returns 32

• Operators with the same precedence are executed from left to right.

BINARY AND HEXADECIMAL NUMBER SYSTEMS

The decimal, binary and hexadecimal number systems all use the same principle. Each digit position in a number represents the power to which the base is raised. The digit in a position is multiplied by the result of the base being raised to its relevant power, and the results of these calculations are added to give the final value. The only difference between the three number systems is the base. The decimal system uses 10, the binary system 2 and the hex system 16.

e.g. decimal

1	2	4
10^2	10^1	10^0

$$= 100 + 20 + 4 = 124$$

binary

1	0	1	1	0	1
2^5	2^4	2^3	2^2	2^1	2^0

decimal equivalent = $32 + 0 + 8 + 4 + 0 + 1$ = 45

When working with hex, the letters A−F are used as the hex equivalents of the decimal number 10−15

e.g.

F	3
16^1	16^0

decimal equivalent = $240 + 3$ = 243

When addresses need to be POKEd into memory (as for the USR function) they must be POKEd a byte at a time even though they are 2 bytes long. To calculate the decimal POKE values for each of the two byte, convert the number into hex, then change the two hexadecimal bytes back to decimal.

e.g.   hex address 1D00

In decimal this is 7424, but you can't POKE this value. So take the high byte (1D) and convert it to decimal

1	D
16^1	16^0

$= 16 + 13 = 29$ POKE Address + 1, 29

now the low byte

0	0
16	16^0
0	0	$= 0$ POKE Address, 0

Logical Operations on Bits

When AND, OR and NOT operands have numeric values they are first converted to 2 byte 2's compliment integers in the range −32768 to 32767. If they are not in this range an error message results.

The logical operation is then carried out on bits. If the operator is AND (or OR) bit 0 of operand 1 is ANDed (or ORed) with bit 0 of operand 2. This is bits of byte 36876 we AND the mask 15 with the byte value. It's easier to see how this works in binary notation.

```
value of 36876     — — — —  1  0  1  0
AND 15             0  0  0  0  1  1  1  1
=                  0  0  0  0  1  0  1  0
```

Because the first 4 bits of the mask are 0, ANDing them will always produce 0 in the first 4 bits of the result, no matter what values were in the first 4 bits of 36876. Because the last 4 bits of the mask are 1, ANDing them will leave the values of the last 4 bits of 36876 unchanged. In general, to make a mask for PEEKing, put a 1 in bit positions you want unchanged, a 0 in those you don't want to know about.

For POKEing 1 into certain bits, an OR mask should be used. For example, to set bit 2 in 36876 OR the mask 4.

e.g. POKE 36876, PEEK(36876) OR 4

Agan, it's easier to see how this works in binary.

```
value of 36876    –  –  –  –  1  0  1  0
OR 4              0  0  0  0  0  1  0  0
=                 –  –  –  –  1  1  1  0
```

To POKE 0 into certain bits, AND a mask with 0 bits in the positions you want set to 0, 1 in those you want left unchanged.

NOTing a byte reverses all the bits values.

```
e.g.  NOT          1  1  0  1  0  1  1  0
      =            0  0  1  0  1  0  0  1
```

Note that reversed characters (inverse video) can be created by NOTing the values of the unreversed character definition bytes.

CHAPTER 2

VIC 20 BASIC Commands

The following describes, in alphabetic order, all the BASIC commands available on the VIC 20. Those that are described as functions return values, like expressions, and can therefore be used where values of the appropriate type can be used. As with expressions, there are exceptions to this. Note that functions appearing in expressions are evaluated before operators, unless the operators are parenthesized

ABS

> : function
> : ABS ([number])
>   ABS ([numeric variable])
>   ABS ([numeric expression])
> : returns the absolute value of its argument ie. positive values are unchanged, negative values become their positive equivalents
>   e.g. ABS (6) returns 6
>   ABS (−72.3) returns 72.3
>   ABS (6+4*−3) returns 6
>   ABS (A%) returns positive magnitude of A%

AND

> : operator
> : [expression] AND [expression]
> : returns true (−1) if both expressions are true
>   returns false (0) if either or both expressions are false
>   e.g. IF X=1 AND Y < =7 THEN GOTO 60
>   IF HIT% AND Z < > 6 THEN GOSUB 70

ASC

> : function
> : ASC ([character string])
>   ASC ([string variable])
> : returns the character code value of the first character in the string
>   e.g. ASC (A) returns 65
>   ASC (BAT) returns 66
>   ASC (A$) returns code of first character of A$
>   ASC ("") null string produces ILLEGAL QUANTITY error

ATN

    : function
    : ATN ([number])
    ATN ([numeric expression])
    : returns the arctangent of its argument in radians. The result is in
    the range $+ \pi /2$ to $-\pi /2$
    e.g. ATN (3) returns 1.24904577
            ATN (6*3 − 15) returns 1.24904577

CHR$

    : function
    : CHR$ ([number])
    CHR$ ([numeric expression])
    The argument to CHR$ must be between 0 and 255.
    : returns the single character string whose code is equal to the
    CHR$ argument
    e.g. CHR$ (65) returns 'A'
           PRINT CHR$(13) will print a RETURN − ie. the cursor will
           act as though the RETURN key has been pressed.
           Colour and reverse mode can also be controlled in this way.

CLOSE

    : statement
    : CLOSE [file−number]
    : closes the file started in an OPEN statement. You should execute
    a PRINT# to that file before closing it, to make sure that all data
    has been transmitted from the buffer.
    e.g. OPEN 1,4 :PRINT#1, END DATA : CLOSE 1

CLR

    : statement
    : CLR
    : This is not equivalent to the CLR key! This statement clears out
    any variables that have been defined, un-DIMensions any arrays
    that have been defined and RESTORES the DATA pointer to the
    beginning of data. It also closes all logical files currently open. The
    commands RUN, LOAD and NEW all automatically execute a
    CLR statement. Note that the program itself is left untouched after
    a CLR statement.
    e.g. 10 A% = 53 : CLR : PRINT A%
           This will display a 0

CMD

    : statement
    : CMD [file-number]
    Normally, the screen is used to display output - i.e. it is the default

output device. The CMD statement changes the default output device to the file number given as argument. This enables you to redirect everything normally displayed by the VIC to, for example, the printer. A CMD statement must be preceded by an OPEN statement. There are 3 ways to exit the CMD mode:

1) Press RUN/STOP and RESTORE keys. This will reset the VIC 20 to its default condition.

2) Use the CMD statement to change the default output. e.g. CMD 3 makes the screen the default.

3) Execute a PRINT# [file−number]. This is preferred since it also empties the printer buffer.

e.g. 10 OPEN 1,4 - opens a channel to the printer
    20 CMD 1 - makes printer default output
    30 LIST - lists the program currently in memory to the printer
    40 PRINT#1 - makes sure the printer buffer is empty, and exits the CMD mode
    50 CLOSE 1 - closes the channel to the printer

CONT

  : statement
  : CONT
  : This continues a program which has stopped due to a STOP keypress, or the execution of a STOP or END statement within a program. CONT will not work if the program stopped due to an error, or if an error is made while the program is stopped, or if any attempt is made to edit the program (even if nothing in the program is actually changed). Variable values may be examined and changed, and the program may be listed.

COS

  : function
  : COS ([numeric expression or variable or constant])
  : returns the cosine of the argument in radians
   e.g. COS (0.4) returns 0.921060994

DATA

  : statement
  : DATA [constant], [constant],...,...,...
  There may be one or more numeric or string constants. String constants need not appear within double quotes, unless the string contains graphics characters, commas, spaces or colons. Two commas with nothing between them will be read as either 0 or the null string, depending on the variable type the data is being read into . DATA statements may appear anywhere in a program. Since they need not be explicitly executed during the running of the program they may appear after an END statement.

: Provides data for a READ statement

   e.g. 10 DATA 6, −73.2, HELLO,"10 DATA", "A.,B"

      20 DATA 7,23,,GOODBYE

: Note: DATA statements cannot be used in immediate mode.

DEF FN

: statement

: DEF FN [name] ([parameter]) = [expressions]

[name] must be a floating point variable name 5 characters or less in length. [parameter] must be a numeric variable name. [expression] must be numeric, user–defined; string functions are illegal. Previously defined functions may appear in [expression]

: defines a function with 1 parameter which may be referenced later in the program

   e.g. 10 DEF FNA (X) = X ↑ 3   - define the function

      20 PRINT FNA (2) - execute the function, replacing the parameter with value 2 result - displays 8 (2 ↑ 3)

      30 PRINT FNA (Z) - replace parameter with value of Z result - displays value of Z ↑ 3

: Note: Can only be used in program mode, although functions defined in program mode may be used in immediate mode.

DIM

: statement

: DIM[variable] ([integer],[integer],...)

: The [variable] identifies the array name and type. The integers indicate the number of elements in each dimension of the array. Since numbering of array elements starts from 0, DIM A(10) defines an array with 11 elements. The number of integers indicates the number of dimensions in the array. DIM A$(4,4) defines a 2 dimensional array of 25 elements. A DIM statement may define more than one array.

   e.g. DIM A$ (6), B (7,2), C% (1,2)

: defines an array. One dimensional arrays of 11 elements may be used without a DIM statement, since the VIC 20 will implicitly define them for you when they are first referenced.

Arrays may be DIMensioned only once (even those implicitly defined).

Only elements of the type specified by the array name may be stored in the array.

   e.g. 10 DIM A$ (10) - defines string array of 11 elements

      20 DIM B% (3,5) - 2 dimensional integer array of 24 elements

      30 DIM C$ (6) , D (7,6,3) - string array - 7 elements and floating point array - 224 elements

      40 PRINT C$ (3) - displays fourth element of array C$

50 D (1,4,2) = 6.2 - assigns 6.2 as value of D (1,4,2)
60 A$ = C$ (1) - assigns value of C$ (1) to A$
(See Data Structures section for details of arrays)

END

: statement
: END
: stops a program and returns control to the user. Doesn't clear variables, array pointers or program, so CONT may be used to continue the program. There may be any number of END statements in a program. Useful for debugging.
e.g. 100 INPUT "CONTINUE", A$
110 IF A$ = "NO" THEN END
—
—
—
200 END

EXP

: function
: EXP ([number])
: returns **e** raised to the power of [number]
e.g. EXP (2) returns 7.3890561

FOR-TO-STEP- / NEXT

: statement
: FOR[variable] = [start] TO [limit] STEP [step] / NEXT [variable]
FOR [variable] = [start] TO [limit] / NEXT [variable]
FOR [variable] = [start] TO [limit] / NEXT
[variable] must be floating point. When STEP is omitted [step] is assumed to be 1. [start], [limit] and [step] may be negative, positive, constants, variables or expressions
: performs a loop through all statements between the FOR and NEXT statements.
A FOR loop is always executed at least once, since the variable value is compared to the limit at the end of the loop.
The loop terminates when the variable value is greater than the limit (if [step] is positive) or less than the limit (if [step] is negative).
FOR loops may be nested to a depth of 10. When nested loops terminate at the same point the NEXT statement may contain more than one variable name. e.g. NEXT I,J,K. In such a case make sure the order is correct. Innermost loops must terminate first.
e.g. 10 FOR J= 7 TO B STEP −3
20 ...
30 ...

40 NEXT J

10 FOR J = 0 TO 6
20 ...
30 FOR K = 0 TO −5 STEP −1
40 ...
50 ...
60 NEXT K, J
Note: When used in immediate mode, a multiple statement line is necessary.
FOR J= 1 TO 5 : PRINT CHR$ (J) : NEXT

FRE

: function
: FRE ([dummy value]) - the value of dummy is unimportant.
: returns the number of free bytes of memory, as is done automatically when the VIC 20 is started.
e.g. PRINT FRE (0)

GET

: statement
: GET [variable]
: checks the keyboard buffer and assigns the first character in it to the variable. If there is nothing in the buffer it assigns the null string to a string variable, or 0 to a numeric variable. The character it GETs is not echoed on the screen. A RETURN keypress is not necessary after typing the character. In fact it will GET a RETURN quite happily, just as it would almost any other character. Since GET doesn't wait for a key to be pressed, it is usually placed in a loop.
e.g. 10 GET A$: IF A$ = " " THEN GOTO 10
15 PRINT "PASSWORD?"
20 GET P$
30 IF P$ = " " THEN 20 − wait for keypress
40 IF P$ = CHR$(13) THEN END − check for RETURN to signal end of password
50 PW$ = PW$ + P$ − build password, character by character in PW$. Note that PW$ starts off as " ", the null string.
60 GOTO 20 − get next character of password
Note: GET cannot be used in immediate mode.

GET#

: statement
: GET# [file−number],[variable]
: same as GET, but gets characters from a previously OPENed

input device such as cassette or disk drive.

e.g. 10 OPEN 1,3
20 FOR J = 1 TO 30
30 GET#1,B$: A$ = A$ + B$
40 NEXT
50 CLOSE 1

This gets a buffer full of data from input device, stops device and then proceeds to read the data from the buffer. In this case it gets the first 30 character from the buffer and builds up the string A$ character by character.

GOSUB/RETURN

Statement

GOSUB [line-number] / RETURN

[line-number] cannot be a variable or expression

: branches to [line-number]. Execution continues from this line until a RETURN statement is read. Then control branches back to the GOSUB statement. Execution continues from the statement after the GOSUB statement.

There may be more than one RETURN statement to cause the branch back to GOSUB. If a RETURN statement is read without a GOSUB first having been executed a RETURN WITHOUT GOSUB error will result. GOSUBs may be nested.

Note: The RETURN statement and the RETURN key are quite different. e.g.   10 GOSUB 560
...
560 IF K$ = "Y" THEN GOSUB 600 : RETURN
570 IF K$ = "N" THEN PRINT "WHY NOT" : RETURN
580 PRINT "ANSWER MUST BY Y OR N"
590 RETURN

...
600 ...

...
75 RETURN

This example shows the use of multiple RETURNs and nesting of GOSUBs. GOSUB 600 is nested inside subroutine 560. GOSUBs may be nested to a greater depth if desired.

(For more on GOSUB see Control Structure section)

GOTO

: statement
: GOTO [line–number]

[line–number] cannot be a variable or expression.

: causes the program to branch to [line-number] if such a line exists. If the line does not exist you get an "UNDEFINED STATEMENT". It is also used in immediate mode to start a program from a particular line. e.g. 10 GOTO 200
...
200 ... — execution continues here

IF – THEN

    : statement
    : IF [condition] THEN [statement(s)]
    [condition] may be logical expression, numeric expression or
    variable name.
    : If the conditions is true the statements after the THEN are
    executed. If the condition is false the THEN statements are
    ignored and execution continues from the next line.
    Logical expression evaluate to -1 (true) or 0 (false). Numeric
    expressions and variables are treated as false if they evaluate to 0
    and as true if they evaluate to any other value.
    When the statement immediately following the THEN is a GOTO
    [line–number], the line–number alone is sufficient.
    e.g. IF A$ = "YES" THEN 70 will execute a GOTO 70 if the
    condition is true.
    e.g. 10 IF (A = 6 OR B = 7) THEN GOSUB 70 : PRINT A$
        20 IF HIT THEN 700 – where HIT is a variable whose value is
        normally 0, but is set to -1 when a collision occurs.
        30 IF NOT(A=7 AND B=4) THEN 70

INPUT

    : statement
    : INPUT [variable list]
    INPUT [string];[variable list]
    [string] must be a string constant, e.g. "PROMPT"
    [variable list] may be 1 or more variables separated by commas
    : where there is no string, the user is prompted for input by a "?".
    Where there is a string, this is printed, followed by ? . INPUT
    differs from GET in that it waits for input, may accept more than
    single characters, echoes input on the screen, and requires a
    RETURN keypress to terminate input. Where the variable list
    contains more than one variable, values must be typed separated
    by commas. The values are assigned to the variables in order. If
    the user types in too few values, the ? reappears and INPUT
    waits for more input. If too many values are typed, the message
    EXTRA IGNORED is displayed. This is not an error and
    execution continues.
    If [string] is too long (the prompt string has a maximum length of 20
    characters), INPUT will read all of the string with the input when
    the input is a string, or return a REDO FROM START otherwise,
    so keep prompts reasonably short. If the user types in a value of
    the wrong type for the variable it is to be assigned to, a REDO
    FROM START message appears, and the user is prompted for
    correct input by "?".
    e.g. 10 INPUT A – displays "?" and waits for a number to be
      typed,   followed by RETURN key.

20 INPUT B, C$ – displays "?", waits for a number followed by a   comma, a string and RETURN key.

30 INPUT "PRICE"; D – displays "PRICE?", waits for number,   RETURN key.

Note: Cannot be used in immediate mode.

INPUT#

: statement

: INPUT# [file – number], [variable list]

: accepts input from an OPENed file by reading that file into the buffer and assigns each data item to a variable in the variable lis, in order. Data items must agree in number and type with the variables in the variable list. If an end – of – record is read before all variables in the variable list have been assigned values, an OUT OF DATA status is generated but the program continues to execute.

INPUT# does not display error messages, it reports error statuses, via the STATUS byte, that the program must respond to.

: because the input buffer is only 80 characters long, an input string, together with separator, cannot be longer than this. Commas and RETURNs act as separators. They cannot act as data – you need a GET# for that.

e.g. 10 OPEN 1,1 – default values used so this OPENs the datatsette

20 INPUT# 1,A$,C,D,E$ – and reads these from buffer.

Note: INPUT# can only be used in program mode.

INT

: function

: INT ([numeric variable, constant or expression])

: returns the largest integer less than or equal to the argument.

e.g. 10 PRINT INT(6.23) – displays 6

20 PRINT INT(-4.2)– displays -5

30 X% = INT(43.4) – assigns value 43 to X%

40 PRINT INT(14) – displays 14

50 PRINT INT(A) – displays integer value of A

LEFT$

: function

: LEFT$ ([string variable, constant or expression], [integer])

: returns a string consisting of the first [integer] characters of the original string argument. If [integer] is greater than the length of the string, the entire string is returned. If [integer] is 0, the null string is returned.

e.g. 10 A$ = "TEST STRING"

20 B$ = LEFT$(A$,4)

30 PRINT B$ – displays "TEST"

40 PRINT LEFT$("GOODBYE",3) – displays "GOO"
50 A$ = LEFT$(A$,3) + LEFT$(A$,4)
60 PRINT A$ – displays "TESTEST"
: LEFT$ is often used to position the cursor. A string of cursor control characters is created which, when printed, moves the cursor across or down the screen. LEFT$ can then be used to control how far across or down the screen the cursor is positioned.
e.g. 10 A$ = "CRSR → CRSR → ..."
20 PRINT LEFT$(A$,10) – moves the cursor across the screen 10 spaces.

LEN

: function
: LEN ([string variable, constant or expression])
: returns the length of the string argument. Blanks and non–printing characters are counted.
e.g. PRINT LEN ("HARRY") - displays 5
10 A$ = "MIGHTY"
20 B$ = LEFT$ (A$,LEN$(A$)–1)
30 PRINT B$ – displays "MIGHT"

LET

: statement
: LET[variable] = [value]
: assigns the value on the right to the variable on the left. The word LET can be omitted, and so is rarely used.
e.g. 10 LET A$ = "HELLO"
20 A$ = HELLO – equivalent to line 10
30 C$ = LEFT(A$,4) – assigns HELL to C$
40 D$ = C$ – assigns value of C$ to D$

LIST

: statement
: LIST – displays entire program
: LIST [line–number] – displays line [line–number]
: LIST – [line–number] – displays from start of program to line [line–number] (inclusive)
: LIST [line–number] — – displays from line [line–number] to end of program
: LIST [line–number1] – [line–number2] – displays from line [line–number1] to [line–number2] (inclusive)
: displays all or part of the program in memory as detailed above. If the program exceeds the length of the screen display, the screen will scroll up. This may be slowed down by holding down the CTRL key, or stopped using the STOP key.

e.g. LIST − 100
      LIST 50 − 999
      LIST 20
: If used in program mode, the program will stop after LISTing.
Typing CONT at this point will only repeat the LISTing.

LOAD

: statement
: LOAD
  LOAD ["filename"]
  LOAD ["filename"],[device]
: transfers a program from cassette or disk into memory.
If there are no arguments to LOAD, the next program found on
tape will be LOADed.
If there is a ["filename"], the VIC 20 will search the tape until a
program of that name is found, and load it. [device] specifies the
device the program is loaded from. If it is 8 , the program will be
loaded from disk, if it is 1, from tape and if it is not present, the
default value is 1, ie tape.
e.g. LOAD − loads next program on tape
      LOAD "MYPROG" − searches tape for program called
      "MYPROG" and loads it if it is found.
      LOAD A$ − searches tape for program whose name is the
      value of A$ and loads it.
      LOAD "*" , 8 − loads first program found on disk.
      LOAD "PR*" , 8 − loads first program whose name begins
      with "PR" from disk.
      LOAD "NB" , 8 − finds program "NB" on disk and loads it.
: When used in immediate mode, a CLR statement is automatically
executed. When used in program mode, if the new program is
shorter than the old one, variables will not be cleared, so the new
program may use the old variable values.

LOG

: function
: LOG ([numeric variable, constant or expression])
: the argument to LOG must be greater than 0
: returns the natural logarithm of the argument, ie. the power to
which e must be raised to give the argument.
e.g. 10 PRINT LOG(6.42856) − displays 1.86075056

MID$

: function
: MID$ ([string variable, constant or expression],[from],[length])
  MID$ ([string variable, constant or expression],[from])
: returns a string of length [length] consisting of the characters
starting from the [from]th character of the string argument. If

[length] is omitted, returns the entire string from the [from]th character on. If [length] is greater than the length of the string argument, the null string is returned.

e.g. 10 PRINT MID$("HELLO",2,3) – displays "ELL"
      20 PRINT MID$("GOODBYE",1,4,) – displays "GOOD"
      30 X$ = "HATTRICK"
      40 PRINT MID$(X$,4) – displays "TRICK"

NEW

    : statement
    : clears program from memory and resets variables
      e.g. X = 6.2
            PRINT X – displays 6.2
            NEW
            PRINT X – displays 0. Old value of X is lost as are any program lines.
    : Using NEW in program mode will clear the program in which it is a program statement.

NOT

    : logical operator
    : NOT [expression or variable]
    : logically negates the truth value of [expression]
    : 10 IF NOT(A=6 AND B=9) THEN 70
    If the expression (A=6 AND B=9) is false then NOT(A=6 AND B=9) is true and the program branches to 70.
    20 IF NOT HIT THEN GOSUB 500
    Assume HIT is a variable set to −1 when a collision between game characters occurs, 0 otherwise. Then NOT HIT will evaluate to true when there is no collision, and the appropriate action (subroutine 500) can be taken.

ON

    : statement
    : ON [variable or expression] GOTO [line−number list]
    ON [variable or expression] GOSUB [line−number list]
    [line−number list] is a series of line−numbers separated by commas
    : causes the program to branch to one of the line−numbers depending on the value of the ON argument. If the argument evaluates to 1, the program branches to the first line−number, if 2 then it branches to the second line−number, etc. If the argument evaluates to 0 or to a number greater than the number of line−numbers then the statement is ignored. If the argument evaluates to a negative number an error occurs.

e.g. 10 ON X%+3 GOTO 50,72,143,90
      20 ON B% GOSUB 70,90,90,300
      30 ON INT(B*C/3) GOTO 20,60,90,15

OPEN

: statement
: OPEN [file−number]
  OPEN [file−number],[device−number]
  OPEN [file−number],[device−number],[command−number]
  OPEN [file−number] , [device−number] , [command−number] ,
  [string]
: OPENs a logical channel for input or output to a device. When a
  channel is OPENed to an external device, a buffer is automatically
  set up. Transmission and receipt of data occurs a whole buffer at a
  time.

  [file−number] is the logical name of the channel, It can be any
  number in the range 1−255, and is the same number used in
  INPUT#, GET#, PRINT# and CLOSE statements to work with
  this device.

  [device−number] specifies the device as below:

Device Number	Device
0	keyboard
1	cassette - default device
2	RS232 device
3	screen
4	printer
5	printer
8	disk drive
4-127	serial bus device
128-255	serial bus device - and send a linefeed (lf) after carriage return.

: [command−number] must be in the range 0−255. The same
  command number will have different effects depending on the
  device specified.

Device	Command Number	Effect
Cassette	0	read tape file
	1	write tape file
	2	write tape file and put EOT (end of tape) marker when channel CLOSEd
Disk	1 - 14	open data channel
	15	open command channel
Keyboard	1 - 255	no effect
Screen	1 - 255	no effect
Printer	0	upper case/graphics
	7	upper/lower case

28

: [string] is sent to the printer or screen as if a PRINT# were performed to the device. With the cassette deck it is used as the filename. With the disk drive it can be either a filename or a command, depending on the command number.

e.g. OPEN 1,0 — open channel to keyboard
OPEN 1,1,0 — open channel to cassette for reading only
OPEN 1,1,0, MYPROG — open channel to cassette for reading only. When a read is done, the VIC 20 will search tape for "MYPROG"
OPEN 1,3 — open read/write channel to screen
OPEN 1,8,15, command — open channel to disk and send command

OR

: logical operator
: [expression] OR [expression]
: produces a true result (−1) if either or both of the expression are true, a false result (0) only if both expression are false
e.g. 10 IF (A=6 OR B$="NO") THEN 90
20 IF (HIT% OR B=6) THEN GOSUB 60

PEEK

: function
: PEEK ([address])
: returns the contents, in decimal, of the byte named by [address]. [address] must be in the range 0 to 65535. A list of memory locations of interest is given in Appendix B.
e.g. 10 PRINT PEEK(36879) — displays the value of the screen background/border colour byte.
20 PRINT PEEK(651) — displays the time a key must be pressed before it repeats automatically

POKE

: statement
: POKE [address],[value]
: puts [value] into the byte at [address]. [value] must be in the range 0 to 255. Unlike PEEK, which will return the contents on any address in memory, POKE can only change the value of RAM (Random Access Memory). In the unexpanded VIC 20 location 0−1023, 4096−8191, 38400−38911, 36864−36879 and some locations in the 6522 chip are RAM. The rest of memory is ROM (Read Only Memory) on which POKE will have no effect.
e.g. POKE 36879,8
10 A=650 : B=128
20 POKE A,B
30 FOR J=0 to 63

```
40 POKE 7168+J, PEEK(32768+J)
50 NEXT J
```
: Lines 30 to 50 copy the first 64 characters from character memory (ROM), starting at address 7168

POS

: function
: POS ([dummy])
the value of the dummy argument may be anything as it's not used.
: returns the cursor's position in a line. Since a logical line may be up to 88 characters long, a value betweeen 0 and 88 may be returned.
If no cursor is being displayed, e.g. during a string manipulation in a program, the position of the character currently being handled is returned. Since a string of up to 255 characters may be built using concatenation, a value in the range 0−255 will be returned.
e.g. PRINT "CURSOR AT"; POS(0) − displays "CURSOR AT 9"

PRINT

: statement
: PRINT [argument]
PRINT [argument], [argument] ...
PRINT [argument]; [argument] ...
: displays the arguments listed after PRINT. If the arguments are separated by a comma, the VIC 20 reserves 11 spaces for the arguments, so displays may be widely separated. if the arguments are separated by semi−colons, there is no separation between arguments.
After each PRINT statement the cursor automatically moves to the next line. This can be stopped by finishing the PRINT statement with a comma or semi−colon.
String arguments to PRINT may contain special characters such as cursor control and colours. These characters appear in the string as reversed characters. (See Appendix C) Where the PRINT statement is executed, the special characters carry out their function. They are not displayed.
"Programmable" cursor controls are CRSR ↑ , CRSR ↓ , CRSR ← , CRSR → , CLR, HOME, INST. Some special characters need different treatment, however. For example, DEL and RETURN operate normally when an attempt is made to put either in a string, and quote marks will terminate the string.
As you have probably found out, pressing DEL deletes a character but you might at some time want to program it into a string. The following steps show how to achieve this:
1) Terminate the string with quotation marks. e.g. "STRING"

2) Press DEL — this will delete the closing quotation marks but leave you out of quote mode.

3) Press INST as many times as you want to insert a DEL, say twice.

4) Now press DEL twice. These DELs will display as reversed characters and will not execute yet.

5) Now put in replacement letters, if any, and complete the string with quote marks.

All your keypresses should look something like this:

"STRING" start with completed string

press DEL to remove quotemark

press INST twice to insert 2 DELs

press DEL twice

Add replacement letters, in this case FE

close quotation marks

The display should now look like this:

e.g. 10 PRINT "STRING ▮ ▮ FE"

and when executed will display "STRIFE"

When LISTed the string looks as it displays, so editing can be difficult if you've forgotten what you've done.

Other special characters can be put into strings in the following way:

(i)   Type the string, and RETURN key, leaving spaces for characters to be added later

(ii)   Use cursor control keys to get back to the space

(iii)   Press CTRL, RVSON

(iv)   Press the keys corresponding to the special character you want, as shown below:

Character	Type
Shift Return	SHIFT M
switch to lower case	N
switch to upper case	SHIFT N
disable case switching keys	H
enable case switching keys	I

: The Shift Return character, like DEL executes when LISTed, so editing will again be difficult.

A more general, easier to remember, and more obvious method of "programming" special characters is to use CHR$ and concatenation.

Note: PRINT can be abreviated to "?"

e.g. PRINT 50

10 PRINT A$, 60; B

20 ? "A STRING" ; 24 ; "LETTERS LONG"

30 PRINT "LATEST PROGRAM"

40 FOR J=0 TO 1000 : NEXT

50 ? "CRSR ↑ CRSR → CRSR → CRSR →
CRSR → "DEL INST INST DEL DEL"

Lines 30−50 will display "LATEST PROGRAM", wait, and change it to "LAST PROGRAM". Line 50 will not look like this when you type it in. As written , it indicates the keys you press.

PRINT#

: statement
: PRINT# [file−number],[variable list]
: similar to PRINT, but sends the contents of the variable list to a device which has been previously OPENed. The variable list is transmitted in the same format as it would be PRINTed to the screen. If commas are used to separate variables, extra spaces are sent, if semi−colons are used, no spaces are transmitted. The commas and semi−colons are not themselves PRINT#ed.

If no comma or semi−colon appears at the end of the variable list a CHR$(13) (RETURN) is sent. It is probably best to separate variables with CHR$(13) on the file so that INPUT$ can be used to read them back.

e.g. 10 OPEN 1,1,1,"Data File"
20 RT$ = CHR$(13)
30 PRINT#1,"LOW SCORE";RT$;LS;RT$;"HIGH SCORE"
40 PRINT#1,"AVERAGE";RT$;A$
50 CLOSE 1

OPENing the file clears the tape buffer ready for data. The buffer retains the data until it is cleared by a statement that does this as a part of its execution, like OPEN. Commas and semi−colons may also be used to separate variables on the file. these must be explicitly PRINT#ed as the RETURNS were in the example above.

READ

: statement
: READ [variable list]
variables in the list are separated by commas
: reads data from DATA statements and assigns each data item to the next variable in the variable list. When there is no unread data in DATA statements and a READ is attempted, an "OUT OF DATA" error occurs and the program aborts.

DATA statements are read in order of ascending line number. Within a DATA statement, data is read sequentially from left to right. The VIC 20 increments a DATA pointer after each element is read. If a RESTORE statement is used, the DATA pointer is reset to point to the first data item of the first DATA statement.

e.g. 20 READ A, C$, B, D$
60 DATA 6.4, HI, 2.6, LO
When new data items are assigned to a variable, the old value is lost.
70 READ C$, C$
80 DATA HI, BYE
Final value of C$ is "BYE"
   90 FOR J=1 TO 5
100 READ A(J) : NEXT
110 DATA 1, 2, 3, 6, 9

REM

: statement
: REM[text]
: no effect — REM statements are ignored by BASIC. They are provided to enable programmers to include comments about the program.
If graphics characters are used in a REM statement they must be preceded by quote marks, otherwise they will be interpreted as BASIC keywords.
REM statements may appear as the last statement on a multiple statement line. If they are not last, any statements following them on the line will be ignored.
e.g. 20 REM 20 – 160 CALCULATE GROSS WAGES
150 GOTO 200 :REM BRANCH TO "HIT" SUBROUTINE

RESTORE

: statement
: RESTORE
: each time a READ is executed, the DATA pointer is advanced to point to the next DATA item. RESTORE resets the DATA pointer to the first data item of the first DATA statement.
e.g.   10 FOR J=1 TO 6
       20 READ A$ (J) : NEXT
       30 RESTORE
       40 FOR J=7 TO 12
       50 READ A$ (J) : NEXT
       60 DATA A, B, C, D, E, F, G

RIGHT$

: function
: RIGHT$ ([string variable, constant or expression],[number])
: returns the string consisting of the rightmost [number] of characters of the original string. If [number] equals the length of the string, the entire string is returned. If [number] equals 0, the null string is returned.

e.g. 10 ? RIGHT$("FRANTIC" , 5) – displays "ANTIC"
    20 ? RIGHT$(A$, LEN(A$)–1) – displays all but the leftmost
    character of A$

RND

    : function
    : RND ([number])
    : returns a pseudo–random number between 0 and 1 (not
    including 1). When [number] is positive, the same
    pseudo–random sequence is generated, no matter what the
    number. When [number] is negative, each number generates its
    own sequence. When [number] is 0, a random number is
    generated from internal clocks.
    e.g. 10 REM SUBROUTINE FOR RANDOM DICE THROW
        20 T1=RND(0) – get random number between 0 and 1
        30 T2=(T1*6)+1 – change to range 1 – 6.9999...
        40 THROW = INT(T2) – get integer value of throw
        This could, of course, be done on one line.
        20 THROW = INT(RND(0)*6)+1

SAVE

    : statement
    : SAVE
    SAVE ["filename"]
    SAVE ["filename"],[device]
    SAVE ["filename"],[device],[command]
    : saves the program currently in memory onto cassette tape or
    diskette.
    If there are no arguments to SAVE, the program is saved to tape
    with no name. If the [filename] is given, the program is saved to
    tape under that name.
    [device]specifies tape (using code 1) or diskette (using code 8).
    [command] may be:
    1)   – when loaded the program will go into the same part of
    memory it came from.
    2)   – an end–of–tape marker will be written after the program.
    When the VIC20 reads this later, it will act as though it has
    reached the end of the tape.
    3)   – combination of 1 and 2.
    e.g. SAVE
        SAVE "GAME1" – saves GAME1 on tape
        SAVE G$ – saves on tape with the value of G$ as name
        SAVE "GAME2",8 – saves "GAME2" on diskette
        SAVE "GAME3",1,1 – saves on tape – will reload into same
        part of memory.

SAVE "GAME4",1,3 – saves on tape – adds EOT marker –
will reload into same part of memory.
Usually used in immediate mode, but can be used in
program mode. The program will continue normally after
SAVEing.

SGN

: function
: SGN ([number])
: if [number] less than 0 returns −1
  if [number] equal to 0 returns 0
  if [number] greater than 0 returns 1
  e.g. 20 IF SGN(X) = 1 THEN 60
         30 ON SGN(X)+2 GOSUB 100, 200, 300

SIN

: function
: SIN ([number])
: returns the sine of the argument, which is in radians
  e.g. 20 ? SIN(1.5) – displays .997494987

SPC

: function
: SPC ([number])
: prints [number] spaces on the screen. [number] must be between
  0 and 255. SPC can only used with PRINT.
: 20 PRINT "LEFT" ; SPC (7) : "RIGHT"
  PRINT SPC (21) ; "!"

SQR

: function
: SQR ([number])
: returns the square root of [number] , [number] must be greater
  than or equal to 0
  e.g. 10 PRINT SQR (4) - displays 2
        20 A = 64
        30 ? SQR (A) - displays 8
        40 ? SQR (A * A) - displays 64

STATUS

: function
: STATUS or
  ST
: returns a value corresponding to the state of the last input/output
  operation. Different bits of the status byte are set on different
  conditions, as shown below:

Bit	Value	Cassette read	Serial Bus R/W	Tape Verify and Load
0	1		time out write	
1	2		time out read	
2	4	short block		short block
3	8	long block		long block
4	16	unrecoverable read error		any mismatch
5	32	check sum error		check sum error
6	64	end of file	EOI	
7	−128	end of tape	device not present	end of tape

```
e.g.  10 OPEN 1, 1, 0, "DATA"
      20 GET# 1, A$
      30 IF STATUS = 64 THEN 60
      40 PRINT A$
      50 GOTO 20
      60 PRINT A$ : CLOSE 1
```

STOP

: statement

: STOP

: halts a program and returns control to the user. The only difference between STOP and END statements is that the STOP statement produces the message "BREAK IN" [line-number]
Thus, with more than one STOP in a program, you can be sure which one has been reached. As with the END statement, variables can be examined and changed and the program continued with CONT.

e.g. 70 STOP - displays "BREAK IN 70" and halts.

STR$

: function

: STR$ ([numeric constant, variable or expression])

: returns the string representation of the value of the argument.

```
e.g.  10 ? STR$ (57.42) - displays "57.42"
      20 ? STR$ (−73) - displays "−73"
      30 ? STR$ (2E + 2) - displays "200"
      40 ? STR$ (3E + 10) - displays "3E + 10"
      50 A = 67.24
      60 ? STR$ (A) - displays "67.24"
```

: Note that positive numbers have a leading space reserved for the sign so when STR$ed they are longer than they look.

e.g. 70 ? LEN (STR$ (72)) - displays 3

SYS

: statement

: SYS [address]

: in effect, performs a GOSUB to the machine language program starting at [address]. This is the most common way to mix BASIC and machine language programs.

The VIC20 already has useful machine language routines (Kernal routines) which can be accessed via SYS. A list of these appears in Appendix D. Also, users may POKE their own machine language routines into memory and access them with SYS.

e.g. 20 SYS 65512 - gets character from keyboard buffer
30 SYS 4400 - jumps to routine previously POKEd into memory at address 4400, and returns.

NOTE: See machine language programming chapter.

TAB

: function

: TAB ([numeric variable, constant or expression])

: moves cursor to the position in a logical line given by the argument. If the cursor is already past that position on the current line, it is moved to that position on the next line. The leftmost position on the screen is 0. The TAB argument must be in the range 0 - 255. TAB must be used with a PRINT statement.

e.g. 20 PRINT "NAME" ; TAB (8) ; "ADDRESS"

TAN

: function

: TAN ([numeric variable, constant or expression])

: returns the tangent of the argument, which is in radians.

e.g. 20 PRINT TAN (1.642)

TIME

: function

: TIME or

TI

: returns the value of an internal clock which counts intervals of one sixtieth of a second (jiffies). This is initialized on start-up and reset to 0 after 51,839,999 increments. This may be useful for timing program segments.

e.g. 20 X = TI : GOSUB 600
30 ET = (TI - X) / 60
40 ? "subroutine 600 took" ;
50 ? ET ; "seconds to execute"

TIME$

: function

: TIME$ or

TI$

: returns a 6 character string indicating hours, minutes, seconds - i.e. "HH MM SS" - on a 24 hour clock. The time must be initialized by the user. It is lost when the VIC20 is turned off.

e.g. 20 TI$ = "131500" - initialize to 1.15 pm.
30 IF TI$ < > "131559" THEN 30
40 ? "WAKE UP"

USR

: function

: USR ([arg])

: calls a user written machine language subroutine, whose starting address is stored at memory addresses 1 and 2 (low byte in 1, high byte in 2). To calculate the POKE values for each address byte, find the address in Hex and convert each byte to decimal (see Graphics chapter for the Hex-Decimal conversion). The [arg] is initially stored in the floating point accumulator (memory locations 97 - 102), and the result returned is the final value stored in the accumulator.

e.g. 20 POKE 1, 0 : POKE 2 , 29 - poke start address (1D00 = 7424)
30 A = USR (3) - call subroutine, assign result to A

VAL

: function

: VAL ([string constant, variable or expression])

: returns the numerical value of the string argument. If the string does not start with +, −, ., or a digit, the function returns 0

e.g. 20 INPUT "PRICE" ; A$
30 PR = VAL (A$)
40 IF PR = 0 THEN PRINT "NUMBER EXPECTED" : GOTO 20
50 ? VAL ("73.2") - displays 73.2
60 ? VAL ("7" + "3" + "." + "2") - displays 73.2
70 ? VAL (STR$ (73.2)) - displays 0, since STR$ returns "[space] 73.2"
80 ? VAL (MID$ (STR$ (73.2), 2)) - displays 73.2

VERIFY

: statement

: VERIFY
VERIFY ["filename"]
VERIFY ["filename"] , [device]

: checks the program on tape or diskette against the program currently in memory, and displays the message "VERIFY ERROR" if they don't match. This is used to ensure that a program has been SAVEd properly. Make a habit of VERIFYing immediately after SAVEing.

When there are no arguments in VERIFY, it checks the next program it finds on tape. When ["filename"] appears as argument, the program of that name is searched for on tape and VERIFYd, if found.

[device] is used to VERIFY a program saved on diskette. As usual [device] is 8 for the disk drive, 1 for cassette (default).

e.g. VERIFY - checks next program on tape
VERIFY "MYPROG" - searches for "MYPROG" on tape and VERIFYs it, if found.
VERIFY "HERPROG", 8 - searches for "HERPROG" on diskette, and VERIFYs it, if found.

: Don't forget to rewind the tape after SAVEing so that the relevant program can be found.

WAIT

: statement
: WAIT [address] , [mask1]
WAIT [address] , [mask1] , [mask2]
: causes the program to wait until the value in [address] changes in a way specified by [mask1] and [mask2].

The value in [address] is bitwise ANDed with the value in [mask1]. If there is a [mask2], the result of the AND is exclusively ORed with the value in [mask2].

Exclusive OR is different to the OR met previously, which is inclusive. Exclusive OR (XOR) only produces a true result when only 1 of its arguments is true, a false result otherwise.

i.e. 1 XOR 1 = 0 - false
1 XOR 0 = 0 XOR 1 = 1 - true
0 XOR 0 = 0 - false

: If the result of the AND and XOR is 0, WAIT continues to wait. If the result is not 0, execution proceeds normally from the statement following the WAIT. This statement is generally used to monitor I/O activities. A novice programmer is unlikely to need it.

e.g. 20 WAIT 160, 144, 128 (160 is 1 byte of the 3-byte jiffie clock which is continually changing its values.).

: This will cause the program to wait until bit 8 of 160 is off (0) or bit 5 is on (1) or both.

(See Graphics chapter for more on bits, bytes and masks.)

CHAPTER 3

Compressing BASIC Programs

Because the unexpanded VIC 20 has only 3.5K bytes of memory available for BASIC programs, it may sometimes be necessary to compress programs. The following is a list of methods you can use to beat memory shortage.

Abbreviating Keywords

Most BASIC keywords can be abbreviated as shown in the table below. Using these does not directly save memory, since keywords are stored as tokens, not the actual word. However, it means that it is possible to put more information on a line, thus reducing the number of line-numbers, which do use extra memory. Abbreviations are expanded to the full word when LISTed.

Multiple statement lines.

These help minimize the number of line-numbers needed. The only limitation is that a multiple statement line should not exceed 88 characters, including colons and RETURN.

Variables.

Keep variable names short.

When a number, word or string is used often in a program, it should be assigned as the value of a variable, which can then be used in its place.

 e.g. 10 A = 36874
   20 POKE A,13 : POKE A,72 : POKE A,16

This has the added advantage of enabling you to squeeze more on a line.

READ, DATA statement

When a repetitive task, such as defining your own character set, needs to be done, it is more memory efficient to use DATA statements to hold the values together with a READ statement in a loop, than to write all the individual repetitions.

 e.g. 10 FOR J = 0 TO 63
   20 READ A,V : POKE A,V : NEXT
   30 DATA 4000, 0, 4001, 48, 4002, 128 ...
   40 DATA ...

rather than

   10 POKE 4000,0 : POKE 4001,48 : POKE 4002,128

   ...
   70 ... POKE 4063,0

Arrays

These can be used for the same purpose as DATA statements. Where possible, use integer arrays rather than floating point arrays, since elements use 2 bytes compared with 5 for floating point elements.

Spaces

The BASIC interpreter does not need spaces in programs, but if used they are stored. Eliminating them therefore saves memory. It also makes programs difficult to read, so this is best done after all debugging.

GOSUB

Using subroutines obviously saves memory, since it saves writing the same section of code several times. You should note however, that GOSUBs can be fairly slow, since it must stack and retrieve addresses.

TAB, SPC

These two functions may be more economical than a string of cursor control commands to position a character on the screen.

REM statements

These may be removed entirely once the program is debugged and read for use. This isn't a great idea, since you may have to examine or change the program at a later date, but it does save space.

Overlays

This involves breaking programs up into sections which are loaded in sequence. For example, many games programs involve defining a new character set. Instead of having 1 program which both defines the character set and runs the game, 2 programs can be written. The first defines the character set and then LOADs the second program, which runs the game, on top of it. Many programs have such initialization tasks to do, and overlays can be useful in these cases - arrays and variables can be defined and given values by one program and used by another. However, a limitation is that the second program must be shorter than the first program otherwise it will overwrite the variable values.

Memory Expansion

Most of the techniques outlined above are not good programming practices, since they make programs far more difficult to follow. The best way out of the memory shortage problem is to buy more memory. It's also the easiest way.

Abbreviations for BASIC keywords

Command	Abbreviation	Command	Abbreviation
ABS	A SHIFT B	OPEN	O SHIFT P
AND	A SHIFT N	PEEK	P SHIFT E
ASC	A SHIFT S	POKE	P SHIFT O
ATN	A SHIFT T	PRINT	?
CHR$	C SHIFT H	PRINT#	P SHIFT R
CLOSE	CL SHIFT O	READ	R SHIFT E
CLR	C SHIFT L	RESTORE	RE SHIFT S
CMD	C SHIFT M	RETURN	RE SHIFT T
CONT	C SHIFT O	RIGHT$	R SHIFT I
DATA	D SHIFT A	RND	R SHIFT N
DEF	D SHIFT E	RUN	R SHIFT U
DIM	D SHIFT I	SAVE	S SHIFT A
END	E SHIFT N	SGN	S SHIFT G
EXP	E SHIFT X	SIN	S SHIFT I
FOR	F SHIFT O	SPC(*	S SHIFT P
FRE	F SHIFT R	SQR	S SHIFT Q
GET	G SHIFT E	STEP	ST SHIFT E
GOSUB	GO SHIFT S	STOP	S SHIFT T
GOTO	G SHIFT O	STR$	ST SHIFT R
INPUT#	I SHIFT N	SYS	S SHIFT Y
LET	L SHIFT E	TAB(*	T SHIFT A
LEFT$	LE SHIFT F	THEN	T SHIFT H
LIST	L SHIFT I	USR	U SHIFT S
LOAD	L SHIFT O	VAL	V SHIFT A
MID$	M SHIFT I	VERIFY	V SHIFT E
NEXT	N SHIFT E	WAIT	W SHIFT A
NOT	N SHIFT O		

* Take care not to put in another left parenthesis.

Appending BASIC programs

So far, whenever you have loaded a BASIC program it has overwritten the program in memory. However, because the VIC 20 relies on pointers to tell it where the start of program memory is, it is possible to load in a program and join it to the program already in memory.

The start of program memory pointer resides at locations 43 and 44. Type PRINT PEEK(43), PEEK(44) in direct mode. On an unexpanded machine you should get 1 and 16. To change the pointer to point to the end of the program currently in memory, type:

POKE 43, PEEK(45) − 2 : POKE 44, PEEK(46)

Now the next program to be loaded will start at the end of the first program. To make the VIC 20 see both programs as one, reset the pointer to the original value. For an unexpanded VIC 20, type:

POKE 43,1 : POKE 44,16

The only restriction to this technique is that the second program to be loaded must have higher line numbers than the program already in memory.

This technique will enable you to save common subroutines independently and add them to programs when needed.

BASIC program storage format

Program lines are sorted from the start of the BASIC user area in order of ascending line numbers. Variable storage starts from the end of the program . Array storage starts from the end of variable storage. String storage starts at the top end of available user memory and works down towards the end of array storage.

The following pointers are used to keep track of storage.

Pointer Address	Use	Default (unexpanded)
43,44	Start of BASIC area	4096
65,66	Current DATA item	—
45,46	End of program	—
47,48	End of variable storage	—
49,50	End of arrays	—
53,54	End of strings	—
51,52	Start of strings	7679

Program lines are compressed before being stored. That is, keywords are tokenized - converted into a one byte code. Each line is then stored in the following format.

Link Address		Line-nr.		BASIC TEXT	End-of-line
Lo-byte	Hi-byte	Lo-byte	Hi-byte		0

The link address points to the start of the next line. The line number is a 2-byte binary number from 1 to 63999. Line numbers in the BASIC text (as arguments of GOTO, GOSUB) are stored in ASCII format - 1 byte per digit. The end of the line is indicated by a 0 byte. The end of the program is indicated by a 00 link address.

VIC 20 BASIC Keyword Codes

Character/ Keyword	Code (decimal)	Character/ Keyword	Code (decimal)	Character/ Keyword	Code (decimal)
end-of-line	0	POKE	151	=	178
unused	1-31	PRINT#	152		179
same as					
CHR$	32-95	PRINT	153	SGN	180
codes		CONT	154	INT	181
unused	96-127	LIST	155	ABS	182
END	128	CLR	156	USR	183
FOR	129	CMD	157	FRE	184
NEXT	130	SYS	158	POS	185
DATA	131	OPEN	159	SQR	186
INPUT#	132	CLOSE	160	RND	187
INPUT	133	GET	161	LOG	188
DIM	134	NEW	162	EXP	189
READ	135	TAB(	163	COS	190
LET	136	TO	164	SIN	191
GOTO	137	FN	165	TAN	192
RUN	138	SPC(	166	ATN	193
IF	139	THEN	167	PEEK	194
RESTORE	140	NOT	168	LEN	195
GOSUB	141	STEP	169	STR$	196
RETURN	142	+	170	VAL	197
REM	143	–	171	ASC	198
STOP	144	*	172	CHR$	199
ON	145	/	175	LEFT$	200
WAIT	146	I	174	RIGHT$	201
LOAD	147	AND	175	MID$	202
SAVE	148	OR	176	unused	203-254
VERIFY	149		177		255
DEF	150				

Codes are interpreted according to this table except when characters are in a string, when CHR$ codes apply. Arithmetic and relational operators are interpreted as keywords unless they appear in a string.

Clearing the keyboard buffer.

If you are using PEEK (197) to find the current keystroke, the keyboard buffer will fill up. Thus, the next time the VIC 20 looks at the keyboard buffer it will find either meaningless or misleading data. This can, under certain circumstances, cause problems. You should therefore be aware that you can clear the keyboard buffer when necessary.

The buffer is located at addresses 631-340.

The number of characters currently in the buffer is held at address 198. The simplest way to clear the buffer is to POKE 0 into 198.

i.e.   POKE 198,0

The keyboard buffer can also be used in a more positive fashion. Program lines can be added and changed from within a program. For example, the following program allows the user to input functions, have them defined using DEF FN and then have them evaluated.

```
10  PRINT "ENTER FUNCTION OF X"
20  INPUT X$
30  POKE 198,2 : POKE 631,13 : POKE 632,13
40  PRINT "[CLR] 100 DEFFNA (X)=" X$ ": RETURN"
50  PRINT "GOTO 60 [HOME]" : END
60  GOSUB 100
70  INPUT "ENTER X";X : PRINT "F(X)="FNA(X) : GOTO 70
```

Explanation

Line 30 : sets the number of characters in the buffer and puts two returns in there.

Line 40 : prints line 100, substituting the input function for X$.

Line 50 : prints GOTO 60, homes the cursor and ends the program.

With the program over, the characters in the keyboard buffer are executed. The first return enters line 100 into the program. The second causes the immediate command GOTO 60 to be executed, thus re-entering the program.

Line 60 : causes the function to be defined.

Line 70 : evaluates the function at points input by the user.

Window Listing

The same technique can be used to create a program which will list programs one line at a time and allow the user to move forwards and backwards through the listing. Mistakes must be noted and corrected **after** exiting from this program.

To use it, append it to the program to be listed, as described in the section on appending BASIC programs, and type RUN 60000

```
60000  SA = PEEK (44) * 256 + PEEK (43) −1 : FL = SA
60002  LN = PEEK (SA + 3) + PEEK (SA + 4) * 256
60003  PRINT "[CLR] [WHT] GOTO 60010" :
       PRINT "LIST" ; LN
60004  POKE 631 , 19 : POKE 632 , 17 : POKE 633 , 144 : POKE
       634 , 13 : POKE 635 , 19 : POKE 636 , 13 : POKE 198 , 6
60005  END
60010  IF PEEK (197) = 5 THEN 60100 : REM TEST FOR '+' KEY
60020  IF PEEK (197) = 61 THEN 60200 : REM TEST FOR '−'
       KEY
60030  GOTO 60010
60100  REM '+' KEY ACTION
```

```
60105  TE = (PEEK (SA + 1) + PEEK (SA + 2) * 256) − 1
60110  IF (PEEK (TE + 1)) PEEK (TE + 2) * 256) <> 0
       THEN SA = TE
60120  GOTO 60002
60200  REM '−' KEY ACTION
60210  IF SA = FL THEN 60002
60220  SA = SA−1 : IF PEEK (SA) = 0 AND PEEK (SA−4) <>
       0) AND PEEK (SA−3) <> 0 THEN 60002
60230  GOTO 60210
```

Before reSAVEing the program reviewed lines 60000-60230 should be deleted to avoid saving the program above as well.

Autonumber

The following program also uses the keyboard buffer in a similar manner. In this case to provide automatic numbering of BASIC program lines. Type RUN 6000ᴜ ᴌo run it.

```
60000  INPUT "START" ; SA
60010  INPUT "INCREMENT" ; IN
60015  POKE 52 , 28 : POKE 56 , 28 : REM PROTECT MEMORY
       WHERE LN STORED
60020  LN=0 : POKE 7679 , 0 : POKE 7678 , 0 : REM SAVE
       VALUE OF LN
60025  PRINT "[WHT] [CLR] 60030 S =";
       SA ; " :I = " ; IN
60027  PRINT "GOTO 60030"
60028  POKE 631 , 31 : POKE 632 , 19 : POKE 633 , 13 : POKE6 34
       , 13 : POKE 198 , 4 : END
60033  LN = PEEK (7678) + PEEK (7679) *256
60040  PRINT S + I * LN : REM PRINT LINE NUMBER
60045  LN = LN + 1 : POKE 7679 , INT (LN/256) : POKE 7678 ,
       LN − INT (LN/256) * 256
60050  GET K$ : IF K$ = " " THEN 60050
60060  PRINT K$
60070  IF K$     CHR$ (13) THEN 60050
60080  PRINT "[WHT] GOTO 60030"
60090  POKE 631 , 31 : POKE 632 , 145 : POKE 633 , 145 : POKE
       634 , 145 : POKE 635 , 145
60100  POKE 636 , 13 : POKE 637 , 13 : POKE 198 , 7 : END
```

Before saving the program written, lines 60000-60100 should be deleted to avoid saving the program above as well.

Worry-free overlays and the keyboard buffer

When overlays were previously mentioned, one of the restrictions was that the overlay had to be shorter than the program it was loaded over. Using the keyboard buffer bypasses this restriction, and makes the use of overlays tidier. The program lines below should be added to the end of a program to be overlaid.

60000 POKE 631 , 78 : POKE 632 , 69 : POKE 633 , 87 : POKE 634
, 13 : POKE 635 , 76 : POKE 636 , 111 : POKE 637 , 13
60001 POKE 638 , 82 : POKE 639 , 117 : POKE 640 , 13 : POKE
198 , 10

These lines POKE into the buffer the abbreviations for the commands NEW, LOAD and RUN, each followed by a RETURN. Thus the old program is cleared out, the overlay loaded in and run, all without the user having to do anything and without the programmer having to worry about the size of the overlay.

Machine Language merge program

Merge program for an unexpanded VIC-20. The machine code routine is totally relocatable. If you wish to locate the routine at an address other than 7601, then lines 10, 20 and 100 should be changed. Line 10 simply lowers the top of memory pointers so that "MERGE" is not clobbered by BASIC. For VIC's with extra RAM, these pointers should be changed. If these pointers are changed, then the address where the routine is located should also be changed (in lines 20 and 100). Examples of "MERGE" for the unexpanded VIC and a VIC with 8K RAM are given.

```
  5 REM FOR UNEXPANDED VIC-20
 10 POKE55, 176 : POKE56, 29 : REM LOWER TOP OF BASIC
 20 MERGE=29*256+177 : REM MERGE=7601
100 S=7601 : FORI=STOS+78 : READX : C=C+X : POKEI, X :
    NEXT
110 IFC : 8785THENPRINT"DATA ERROR!!" : END
120 DATA169,0,133,10,32,209,225,165
130 DATA43,72,165,44,72,56,165,45
140 DATA233,2,133,43,165,46,233,0
150 DATA133,44,169,0,133,185,166,43
160 DATA164,44,169,0,32,213,255,176
170 DATA14,134,45,132,46,32,51,197
180 DATA104,133,44,104,133,43,96,170
190 DATA201,4,144,244,240,10,104,133
200 DATA44,104,133,43,24,108,0,3
210 DATA164,186,136,240,209,208,239
```

For a VIC with 8K RAM, change lines 5, 10, 20 and 100 to:

```
  5 REM FOR VIC-20 WITH 8K RAM PACK
 10 POKE55,176 : POKE56,29 : REM LOWER TOP OF BASIC
 20 MERGE=63*256+172 : REM MERGE=16300
100 S=16300 : FORI=STOS+78 : READX : C=C+X : POKEI,X :
    NEXT
```

For memory configurations other than the unexpanded and 8K VIC, the pointers should be changed accordingly. To use the routine, first type in the program and then save it as "MERGE". Then, if you intend to merge programs, load and run "MERGE" (this will store the machine code routine). It is now possible to MERGE a program on the end of any program already in memory (if you MERGE and there is no program in memory, then it is the equivalent of a LOAD). The syntax for the merge command is almost identical to the format for the LOAD command:

The format is SYS MERGE "filename", device number

A secondary address may be specified but it will be ignored. For the unexpanded VIC, MERGE=7601 and for a VIC with an 8K RAM pack, MERGE=16300.

CHAPTER 4

GRAPHICS

As you probably already know, the VIC 20 has graphics capabilities available directly from the keyboard, using the graphics characters, colour control keys, cursor control keys and PRINT statements. However, it also has more powerful graphics capabilities available through direct user control of sections of the memory.

Graphics Memory

There are three blocks of memory used to control graphics on the VIC 20 — screen memory, colour memory and character memory — and a few odd bytes we'll discuss as we get to them. First, a brief description of the three blocks, then a more detailed coverage of how to use them.

Screen memory consists of one byte for each character position on the screen. Since the screen has 506 character positions — 23 rows of 22 characters — screen memory has 506 bytes. Actually 512 bytes are allocated, but 6 are unused. The first 22 bytes of screen memory correspond to the first row on the screen, the second 22 bytes correspond to the second row, and so on.

Colour memory, like screen memory, consists of 1 byte for each screen character position. Each byte contains a code for the colour in which characters will be displayed at that postion.

Character memory contains the coded representations of all printable characters. It is broken into 2 blocks - one for upper case and graphics characters, the other for lower and upper case characters.

To display a character on the screen, the VIC 20 finds the code for the character in screen memory, uses the code as a pointer to the character representation in character memory, finds the colour of the character position in colour memory and uses all this information to display the character.

For example, suppose there is a code of 1 at 7680 - the first location in screen memory. The VIC 20 reads the character colour from the corresponding location in colour memory, in this case 38400 - the first location in colour memory. The character representation is found in character memory using the formula:

Start-of-character-memory + (code*8)

in this case

32768 + (1*8) = 32776

The VIC 20 uses the information in 32776 and the next seven bytes to create the character shape, which, in this case, is an 'A'.

LOW RESOLUTION GRAPHICS

Screen Background and Border Colours.

These colours are controlled by the value in byte 36879. The values for background/border colour combinations are given in Appendix E.

e.g.   POKE 36879,79 gives a purple screen and a yellow border.

Character Colour

Keyboard Control

As previously mentioned, the colour of characters can be dictated using the colour control keys. These keys can be included in strings within a program. They change the value in byte 646. This value can also be changed by POKEing.

Changing this value causes everything after the change to be printed in the colour set, i.e. it changes character colour from then on. From this it follows at you must change this value every time you want to change character colour just as you do when using the colour control keys.

Colour Memory Control

You can also POKE values into colour memory thus controlling the colour of indvidual character positions on the screen. This determines the colour of characters POKEd into screen memory, but not characters which are PRINTed. These are controlled by byte 646.

Colour data appears to be stored in different parts of memory, depending on whether the memory has been expanded or not. To find the start of colour memory on your machine use the following formula:

CM=37888 + 256 * (PEEK(648) AND 2)

This will assign the starting address of colour memory to CM.

You may now determine the colour of characters POKEd into screen memory by POKEing the desired values into the relevant bytes of colour memory

0	— Black	4	— Purple
1	— White	5	— Green
2	— Red	6	— Blue
3	— Cyan	7	— Yellow

e.g.   10 CM = 37888 + 256 * (PEEK (648) AND 2)
       20 FOR J = CM TO CM + 506
       30 POKE J , 7 : NEXT

Multicolour Mode

In the VIC 20 the standard mode allows for the characters to be displayed in one colour, the 'foreground colour', against a background of a second colour, the 'foreground colour', whilst the border around the display is in a third colour, the 'border colour'.

In this mode the 'auxiliary colour' is not used. However, the 'multicolour' mode allows the user to have four colours in the display at the same time. There is though one minor handicap with multicolour and that is the resolution of the display is changed from its normal 176x184 to 88x184.

In order to understand the working of the multicolour mode it is necessary to consider the 'character representation' of the character in a different way from that considered in the standard mode. When a bit is set, the 'foreground' colour is chosen, and when reset the 'background' colour is chosen. In the multicolour mode the 'character representation' is considered, for a standard sized character, as a 4 by 8 array, where each element is two bits in size. Then, if the two bits are '00' the 'background' colour is chosen, if '01' the 'border' colour is chosen, if '10' the 'foreground' colour is chosen and if '11' the 'auxiliary' colour is chosen.

The 'multicolour' mode is really intended for use with 'user defined' characters and with colour video monitors that have the ability to display 'multicolour' character accurately. Nevertheless, it is quite feasible to demonstrate 'multicolour' using the standard characters of the character generator ROM. Of these characters 'U' is preferred as it has all four of the two-bit representations that are used in the 'multicolour' mode.

Example: The character representation for 'U'.
The eight bytes of this character are:
66, 66, 66, 66, 66,66, 60, 0
which in binary are:

```
    0 1 0 0 0 0 1 0
    0 1 0 0 0 0 1 0
    0 1 0 0 0 0 1 0
    0 1 0 0 0 0 1 0
    0 1 0 0 0 0 1 0
    0 1 0 0 0 0 1 0
    0 0 1 1 1 1 0 0
    0 0 0 0 0 0 0 0
```

In 'standard mode' this character will be in two colours, the foreground colour F, and the background colour B.

```
B F B B B B F B
B F B B B B F B
B F B B B B F B
B F B B B B F B
B F B B B B F B
B F B B B B F B
B B F F F F B B
B B B B B B B B
```

Whereas in 'multicolour mode' it will be in four colours. The foreground colour F, the background colour B, the border colour b, and the auxiliary colour A.

```
b B B F
b B B F
b B B F
b B B F
b B B F
b B B F
B A A B
B B B B
```

It is important to appreciate that on a VIC20 it is possible to have any number of characters in multicolour mode at a time as all that is required is for the user to set bit 3 of the appropriate locations in the Colour RAM. The following program demonstrates the full range of colour combinations that are possible on a standard VIC20.

PROGRAM: Colour demonstration — standard and multicolour.

```
 10 PRINT CHR$ (147) [clear the screen]
 20 INPUT "foreground (0-7)" ; FR [The user specifies each of the four
colours to be used]
 30 INPUT "BORDER (0-7)" ; BR
 40 INPUT "BACKGROUND (0-15)" ; BA
 50 INPUT "AUXILIARY (0-15)" ; AU
 60 PRINT
 70 INPUT "PRESS RETURN" ; A$ [Wait for user]
 80 PRINT CHR$ (145) ; CHR$ (145) [Cursor up twice]
 90 POKE 36879 , PEEK (36879) AND 8 OR BA*16 [Set background]
100 POKE36879,PEEK(36879) AND 248 OR BR AND 7 [Set border]
110 POKE36878,AU*16[Set auxiliary]
```

```
120 FORD=1 TO 500 [Delay loop]
130 NEXT D
140 FORA=154 TO 307 [Middle third of screen to be 'standard' 'U's]
150 POKE7680+A,21
160 POKE38400+A,FR
170 NEXT A
180 FORA=308 TO 505 [Lower third of display to be 'multicolour' 'U's]
190 POKE7680+a,21
200 POKE38400,FROR8
210 NEXT A
220 INPUT "PRESS RETURN" ; A$ [Wait for user]
230 RUN [Again]
```

Screen Memory

Screen memory is located at different addresses depending on whether memory is expanded or not. To find the start of screen memory, use the following formula:

$$SM = 256*PEEK (648)$$

Byte 648 contains the number of ¼K bytes from 0 to screen memory address.

The simple way to calculate the address of the bytes in screen memory you want to POKE is to use the formula – SM + (row*22) + column. Where SM is the start of screen memory, 'row' is the screen row number (0 is the top row) and 'column' is how far along the row (also starting from 0 at the left of the screen).

Graph paper is handy for working out screen displays.

The values POKEd into screen memory act as pointers into character memory. The are NOT the ASCII values of the characters. The screen codes corresponding to ASCII values are shown below:

ASCII value	Screen value
0-31	None – not displayable
32-63	32-63
64-95	0-31
96-127	64-95
128-159	None – not displayable
160-191	96-127
192-254	64-126
255	94

You will notice that some screen codes are shared by two ASCII codes. This is because character memory is broken into two blocks. The character displayed by a screen code corresponding to two ASCII codes will depend on which block of characters is being used. The screen code, as was mentioned, acts as a pointer into the block of character memory. (see Character Memory section for more details.)

A table of ASCII and screen codes for the two character sets is given in Appendix A. When you know in advance what characters are to be POKEd into screen memory, this table may be used to look up the screen values. However, for some applications, such as GETting characters from the keyboard, the characters can not be known in advance. The ASCII codes convert in blocks of 32 so the screen codes may be calculated using the following subroutine:

```
 10 GET K$
 20 SC = ASC (K$)
 30 ON INT (SC/32) +1 GOTO 40 , 50 , 60 , 70 , 80 , 90 , 100
 40 SC = -1 : RETURN
 50 RETURN
 60 SC = SC-64 : RETURN
 70 SC = SC-32 : RETURN
 80 SC = -1 : RETURN
 90 SC = SC-64 : RETURN
100 IF SC = 255 THEN SC = 94 : RETURN
101 SC = SC-128 : RETURN
```

This subroutine returns −1 when the character is not displayable. The main program can then decide what to do with it.

The following example program POKEs red 'A's into the top half of the screen, green 'Z's into the bottom half:

```
10  REM Set up colour memory
20  CM = 37888 + 256 * (PEEK (648) AND 2)
30  REM Red character positions
40  FOR J = 0 TO 252
50  POKE CM + J , 2 : NEXT
60  REM Green character positions
70  FOR J - 253 TO 505
80  POKE CM + J , 5 : NEXT
90  SM = 256 * PEEK (648)
```

```
100  REM Poke A's into first half of screen memory
110  FORJ= 0 TO 252
120  POKE SM + J , 1 : NEXT
130  REM Poke Z's into second half
140  FORJ= 253 TO 505
150  POKE SM + J , 26 : NEXT
160  GOTO 160 : REM Wait for STOP keystroke
```

Screen shrink/expand

The following effect is produced by changing the number of rows and columns in the screen display and shifting its origin. The screen shrinks and expands. This could be used to distract a user while a new display is poked or printed onto screen memory.

Relevant memory locations.

36864	bits 0 - 6 control horizontal centering - normally 12
36865	controls vertical centering - normally 38
36866	bits 0 - 6 control number of columns - normally 150
36867	bits 1 - 6 control number of rows - normally 46

```
10  FOR J = 1 TO 21
20  POKE 36866, 150-J : POKE 36867, 46-J * 2 : POKE 36864, 12
    + J : POKE 36865, 38 + J * 2
30  FOR K = 0 TO 100 : NEXT K
40  NEXT J
50  FOR J = 21 TO 0
60  POKE 36866, 150-J : POKE 36867, 46-J * 2 : POKE 36864, 12
    + J : POKE 36865, 38 + J * 2
70  FOR K = 0 TO 100 : NEXT J
80  NEXT J
```

Character Memory

Before going into the VIC's character memory it would be worthwhile to first have a look at the character table and then follow this with the memory and how to use it in designing your own characters.

The Character Table

The standard character generator of the VIC20 is a 4K ROM chip that occupies the block of memory from $8000-$8FFF. This ROM holds the 8*8 matrix representations of all the characters that can be displayed on the TV screen. A single character requires 8 locations, each holding 8 bits, in order to have all its points defined.

In the VIC20 system there are a possible 128 different characters and the first 1K of the 4K ROM holds the straightforward representations for each character. The second 1K holds the 'inverse' representations.

In order to get lower case letters it has been necessary to have another 2K of representations of the characters. Once again the first 1K holds the straightforward representations and the second 1K the 'inverse' representations.

The following two simple BASIC programs show the character set of the VIC20 in two different ways:

PROGRAM: Simple display of the standard character set.

```
10FORA=0 TO 255 [Each character in turn]
20POKE38400+A,0 [The colour – black]
30POKE7680+A,A [Display each character. NOTE: Unexpanded VIC20]
40NEXT
run
```

Then use 'shift' and ' ◖▮ ' to get lower case representations.

The second program PEEKs the actual locations and reproduces the data bit by bit. Whenever the bit is set then the program prints a '0' and when the bit is reset the program prints a space.

Program: The character set enlarged 64 times.

```
 10  FOR A=32768 TO 36856 STEP 8   [Each character]
 20  PRINT CHR$(147)   [Clear the screen]
 30  FOR B=A TO A+7   [The eight locations]
 40  LET C=PEEK(B)   [Fetch the data]
 50  FOR D=7 TO 0 STEP −1   [Test each bit]
 60  IF C AND 2 ↑ D THEN PRINT "O";:GOTO 80 [Print "O" if set]
 70  PRINT " "; [Print "(space)" if reset]
 80  NEXT
 90  PRINT
100  NEXT
110  PRINT
120  INPUT "PRESS RETURN";A$   [Wait for key-press]
130  NEXT
RUN
```

The above program will show each of the 512 representations in the character generator ROM, one by one.

In the VIC20 system it is both possible to change the area of memory that is used to hold the character table and to change the character representation from the normal 8 * 8 matrix to one of 8 *16. The second feature will be discussed in the hardware section where different registers within the VIC are discussed.

The first block of character memory — upper case and graphics — occupies the ROM locatons 32768-34815. The second block — lower and upper case — occupies ROM locations 34816-36863.

Characters are displayed as patterns of dots. Each character position on the screen is composed of an 8 × 8 square of dots (pixels). Character memory contains the information which tells the computer which dots to turn on or off for a particular character. If a bit is 1, the dot is on (displayed in character colour). If it is 0, the dot is off (displayed in background colour). Therefore, to cover 64 dots, each character representation takes 8 bytes of memory.

e.g. The character 'A"

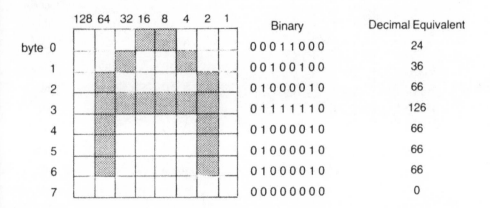

	128 64 32 16 8 4 2 1	Binary	Decimal Equivalent
byte 0		0 0 0 1 1 0 0 0	24
1		0 0 1 0 0 1 0 0	36
2		0 1 0 0 0 0 1 0	66
3		0 1 1 1 1 1 1 0	126
4		0 1 0 0 0 0 1 0	66
5		0 1 0 0 0 0 1 0	66
6		0 1 0 0 0 0 1 0	66
7		0 0 0 0 0 0 0 0	0

As mentioned earlier, the screen codes act as pointers into character memory. As you can see from the table in Appendix A the screen code for A in character set 1 is 1. Its 8 byte representation is therefore stored in:

32768 + (8*1) = 32776 and the next 7 bytes

so byte 32776 contains the value 24
so byte 32777 contains the value 36
so byte 32778 contains the value 66
so byte 32779 contains the value 126
so byte 32780 contains the value 66
so byte 32781 contains the value 66
so byte 32782 contains the value 66
so byte 32783 contains the value 00

In general, to find the starting address of the representation of a character with screen code X use:

32768 + (8*X)   for character set 1
34816 + (8*X)   for character set 2

You can change from one character set to the other from the keyboard as described earlier, or by changing the value of the character memory pointer — byte 36869. Its value is normally 240 (upper case and graphics) or 242 (upper and lower case).

Designing your own characters

Since the built-in character sets are in ROM you cannot directly change them. However, as you have seen, the character memory pointer can be changed. So the secret to using a character set you design yourself is to change the pointer to point to your set.

First, however, you must design your characters. Take a piece of graph paper (or draw an 8 × 8 grid), and for each special character you want, set it up as below. As an example, our grid contains a hat character.

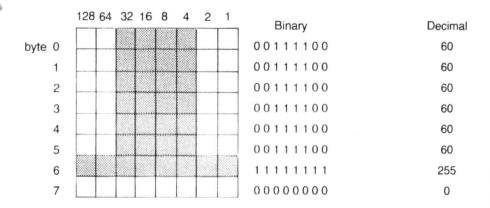

	128 64 32 16 8 4 2 1	Binary	Decimal
byte 0		0 0 1 1 1 1 0 0	60
1		0 0 1 1 1 1 0 0	60
2		0 0 1 1 1 1 0 0	60
3		0 0 1 1 1 1 0 0	60
4		0 0 1 1 1 1 0 0	60
5		0 0 1 1 1 1 0 0	60
6		1 1 1 1 1 1 1 1	255
7		0 0 0 0 0 0 0 0	0

Fill in the squares to create the character you want. Then, for each row, add up the values of the squares filled in. The sum is the value you will POKE into the byte.

It is usual to copy some of the built in character set into RAM and then change those characters you wish to.

A sample exercise should clarify this.

Type POKE 36869, 255

All characters on the screen should now turn to random dots, since the character memory pointer now points to an area of memory where no characters have been defined — the bytes here contain random values. STOP RESTORE will return you to the normal character memory.

Now run the following program:
```
10 POKE 36869,255
20 POKE 52,28 : POKE 56,28 : CLR
30 FOR J = 0 TO 511
40 POKE 7168+J, PEEK (32768+J)
50 NEXT
60 PRINT "A"
70 FOR J = 7176 TO 7183 : READ V : POKE J,V : NEXT
80 DATA 60, 60, 60, 60, 60, 60, 255, 0
```

Explanation:

Line   10— changes the character memory pointer — character memory now starts at 7168

        20— makes sure that BASIC doesn't overwrite the character set

   30-50— copies the first 64 characters (512 bytes) from character set 1 in ROM to RAM, starting at 7168

        60— prints an 'A'

        70— changes the definition of 'A' in character memory to a hat

        80— Data statement holding the values of the new definition of 'A'

Note that all A's displayed on the screen change.
As you can see, there are 3 things you must do to use your own character set:
(i) Change character memory pointer
(ii) Ensure that BASIC doesn't overwrite your character set
(iii) POKE in the new character representations.

Accessing both custom and built-in character sets

If you have redesigned most of the characters in your custom character set, displaying understandable messages can be a problem.
One solution to this makes use of the fact that the VIC chip sees addresses differently to the rest of the computer. If you place the custom character set at 7168-7679, then printing RVSON within a string will cause the VIC chip to access the unreversed character set in ROM when printing that string.
e.g.
```
10 FOR J = 7168 TO 7679
20 REM POKE IN CUSTOM CHARACTERS
— —
40 PRINT "A" — Prints custom character corresponding to A
50 PRINT "[RVS ON] UNREVERSED ROM" — Prints
"UNREVERSED ROM"
```

The reasons for this are as follows:

The VIC chip can only access 16384 bytes, which it sees as a contiguous block from 0 to 16383. To it the location of the custom character set is 15360. Since RVS ON sets the high bit of a character's screen code, all reversed characters have screen codes of 128 up. To access a character with code 128 the VIC chip goes to location 15360 + (128*8) = 16384. Since the VIC chip cannot access 16384 the address "overflows" and wraps around to 0, which the VIC chip sees as the address of the start of character ROM.

Where to put the new character set

A safe (but not the only) place to put character memory is at 7168. This gives you room to put in 64 characters before you run into screen memory, which starts at 7680 on the unexpanded VIC20. To do this POKE 36869,255.

To ensure that BASIC doesn't overwrite your character set you must change the pointers to the end of BASIC program memory and the end of string storage memory. If you are starting character memory at 7168, you can protect it by using:

POKE 52,28 : POKE 56,28 : CLR

This should be done before any BASIC variables are defined or referenced, otherwise BASIC may not recognise the limitation.

Having done the above, you may now POKE in your new character set, starting at 7168. Remember that screen codes act as pointers into character memory, so if you POKE a value of 7 into screen memory, the eighth character in the set will be displayed.

For those who wish to put character memory elsewhere, or use a larger set, the following details will be useful.

In fact, both screen and character memory pointers can be changed. Byte 36869 controls both. The first 4 bits gives the number of K (1024) bytes from 0 to the start of screen memory. The last 4 bits gives the number of K bytes from 0 to the start of character memory.

However, to complicate matters, both of these numbers are calculated using addresses as seen by the Video Interface Chip. It uses different addresses to the rest of the computer to access the same locations. The table below illustrates the differing addresses for the memory blocks the VIC chip can access.

VIC chip addresses	Ordinary addresses	Memory
0	32768	Unreversed Character ROM
1024	33792	Reversed Character ROM
2048	34816	Unreversed upper/lower case ROM
3072	35840	Reversed upper/lower case ROM
4096	36864	VIC and VIA chips
5120	37888	Colour memory
6144	38912	Reserved for expansion
7168	39936	Reserved for expansion
8192	0	System memory
9216	1024	Reserved for expansion
122288	4096	Program
15360	7168	Screen

Screen memory location is also controlled by the '128' bit in byte 36866. If it is set the upper half of the 1K reserved for screen memory is used, otherwise the lower half is used. This could be used as a quick way of switching screens. While the screen memory pointer is pointing to the screen at 7680, a screen memory starting at 7168 can be built, and vice versa. Simply clearing or setting bit 7 of 36866 would change the screen displayed. This could be helpful in games where a part of the screen needed to be changed. Rather than clearing the screen and building a new display - which can be time-consuming - the display can be instantly switched. Normally, this bit is set, so screen memory actually starts at 7680, which is why we can put character memory at 7168. The other bits of 36866 indicate the number of screen columns.

Example calculation of value of byte 36869. To put screen memory at 7680, character memory at 7168:

Address	VIC chip address	No. of K from 0
Screen - 7680	15872	15872/1024 = 15.5
Character - 7168	15360	15360/1024 = 15

Indicate the .5 in the screen memory pointer by setting bit 7 in 36866 - POKE 36866, 150 - and discard it.

Binary representation of byte 36869	Screen mem	Char mem	
	1111	1111	= 255

To calculate it in decimal, use:
(16 * Screen memory pointer) + Character memory pointer
(16 * 15) + 15 = 255
So, POKE 36869, 255

To calculate the POKE values of bytes 52 and 56, work out the number of ¼K bytes (256) from 0 to the start of character memory. Use ordinary addresses, not the VIC chip addresses.

In this example it is 7168/256 = 28

so POKE 52, 28 : POKE 56, 28 : CLR

Bytes 55, 56 indicate the end of BASIC program memory.

Bytes 51, 52 indicate the start of BASIC string storage.

Bytes 51 and 55 are 0 after a CLR or RUN and so can be ignored.

Some programs, such as the Programmer's Aide, check byte 644 instead of 55, 56 to find the end of BASIC memory. To avoid these overwriting your character set you should POKE the same value into 644, if you're using such a program.

HIGH RESOLUTION GRAPHICS

In low resolution graphics, characters are the focus of attention. You define characters, you move characters around and so on. In high resolution graphics the dots (pixels) which make up the characters are the focus of attention. The difference between the two is in programming technique, not in the way in which things are displayed.

Typically, in low resolution, the character set, once defined, is not changed, while the screen memory is. In high resolution, screen memory, once defined, is not changed, while character memory is. The trick is to think of character memory not as defining characters, but as defining the screen - one bit in character memory controlling one pixel on the screen.

Unfortunately the standard VIC20 does not have enough memory to define the entire screen. However it is possible to map part of the screen as follows:

First we set up our screen map (character memory), protect it from BASIC and clear it.

```
10 POKE 36869, 255
20 POKE 52, 28 : POKE 56, 28 : CLR
30 FOR J = 7168 TO 7679
40 POKE J , 0 : NEXT
```

Next we set up the high resolution area.

```
50 SV = 0
60 FOR J = 7680 TO 7855 STEP 22
70 FOR K = 0 TO 7
80 POKE J + K , SV : SV = SV + 1
90 NEXT K , J
```

This creates a 64 x 64 pixel area at the corner of the screen. On this area,

BYTE = SC + INT(Y/16) * 352

Now, to change a pixel, we merely need to change the bit in character memory corresponding to it. If we consider the high resolution work area as a 64 × 64 grid:

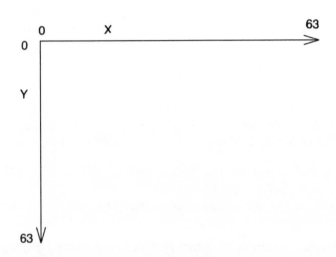

we can give any pixel X and Y co-ordinates and work out the bit to change as follows:

CHAR = INT (X/8)
ROW = INT (Y/8)
BYTE = 7168 + ROW * 64 + CHAR * 8 + (Y - INT (Y/8) * 8)
BIT = 7 - (X - (CHAR * 8))

To turn 1 bit on while leaving the other bits in the byte unchanged, OR a mask with the current value of the byte.

e.g. POKE BYTE, PEEK (BYTE) OR (2 ↑ BIT)

Suppose we want to turn on the pixel with co-ordinates (35, 32). For the sake of the example assume the relevant byte has a value of 47. Using the formulae above we get:

POKE 7456, PEEK (7456) OR 2 ↑ 4

```
          2↑4  0 0 0 1 0 0 0 0
OR PEEK (7456)  0 0 1 0 1 1 1 1
          ─────────────────────
        gives   0 0 1 1 1 1 1 1
```

To turn off a bit, AND NOT a mask with the current value of the byte

e.g. POKE BYTE, PEEK (BYTE) AND NOT (2 ↑ BIT)

To turn off the bit we just turned on

POKE 7456, PEEK (7456) AND NOT (2 ↑ 4)

```
            2↑4  0 0 0 1 0 0 0 0
        NOT 2↑4  1 1 1 0 1 1 1 1
AND PEEK (7456)  0 0 1 1 1 1 1 1
          ───────────────────────
          gives  0 0 1 0 1 1 1 1
```

Mapping the entire screen

Even if you have enough memory to map the entire screen, at first glance it seems as though there are not enough screen codes to map the entire screen. The solution to this problem is to use double height characters. In this mode each screen code acts as a pointer to 16 bytes in character memory, rather than 8. Double height mode is controlled by bit 0 of 36867.

To set double height mode:

POKE 36867, PEEK (36867) OR 1

To set normal height mode:

POKE 36867, PEEK (36867) AND 254

Since characters are now 16 bytes high, the formulae to access the bit requiring setting to turn on a screen pixel differ slightly, as below.

BYTE = SC + INT (Y/16) *352 + INT (X/8) *16 + (Y-INT (Y/16) *16)
BIT = 7 - (X - INT (X/8) * 8)
(where SC is the start address of custom character memory)

The following example program plots a sine curve on the high resolution area.

```
 10  POKE 52, 28 : POKE 56, 28 : CLR
 20  FOR J = 7168 TO 7679 : POKE J , 0 : NEXT
 30  POKE 36869, 255
 40  POKE 36879, 8 : REM Border/Background colour
 50  PRINT CHR$ (147) : SV = 0
 60  FOR J = 7680 TO 7855 STEP 22
 70  FOR K = 0 TO 7
 80  POKE J + K, SV : SV = SV + 1
 90  NEXT K, J
100  FOR X = 0 TO 63
110  Y = 32 + SIN (X/4) * 20 : GOSUB 200
120  NEXT X
130  GOTO 130
200  BYTE = 7168 + INT (Y/8) * 64 + INT (X/8) * 8 + (Y - INT
     (Y/8) * 8)
210  BIT = 7 - (X - INT (X/8) * 8)
220  POKE BYTE, PEEK (BYTE) OR (2 ↑ BIT)
230  RETURN
```

Unfortunately, BASIC is too slow for most high resolution applications. It is generally better to use machine language programs which are many times faster.

Multicolour Characters

So far, each character position has been restricted to 2 colours - background and character. At the expense of resolution, it is possible to add two more colours - border and auxiliary.

Instead of a character position being 8 × 8 dots, in multicolour mode it is 4 × 8 dots - i.e. it takes 2 bits to define a dot, which is now 2 pixels wide. e.g.

screen dot	3	2	1	0
character byte	1 0	0 0	0 1	1 1

The colours selected by each 2 bits are as follows:

Bit pair   Colour
0 0   Background
0 1   Character colour
1 0   Border colour
1 1   Auxiliary colour

When designing multi-coloured characters, the POKE values for character memory are calculated exactly as for normal characters.

You know how to set background, border and character colours. The auxiliary colour can be any of the 16 background colours - the following codes apply:

0 - Black	8 - Orange
1 - White	9 - Light Orange
2 - Red	10 - Pink
3 - Cyan	11 - Light Cyan
4 - Purple	12 - Light Purple
5 - Green	13 - Light Green
6 - Blue	14 - Light Blue
7 - Yellow	15 - Light Yellow

It is set by POKEing the relevant value * 16 into byte 36878. However, it only uses the top 4 bits, the others are used by the sound generator. If you wish to avoid changing the sound generator value use a mask, as below:
    POKE 36878, (PEEK (36878) AND 15) OR (16 * AUX-CODE)
However, if you are not using sound at the same time as multicolour graphics, just POKE 36878, 16 * AUX-CODE.

The VIC20 must be made to interpret character memory bytes as multicoloured. To do this, the 4th bit in each colour memory byte that you want multicoloured must be set to 1. So when you POKE the colour codes into colour memory add 8 to the normal codes. The same technique applies to characters PRINTed. POKEing the usual code + 8 into byte 646 will make the VIC20 interpret character codes as multicoloured characters when PRINTing.

The auxiliary colour is initially set to black. Multicolour and normal resolution characters may be mixed by setting the 4th bit on some colour memory nybbles and not on others.

CHAPTER 5

SOUND

The VIC20 also has sophisticated sound generating capabilities. It has 3 tone registers covering 5 octaves, a white noise generator and volume control.

Sound is very easy to use. There are simply 5 memory locations into which you POKE values.

Address	Use	Admissable values
36874	Low range tones	128 - 255
36875	Mid range tones	128 - 255
36876	High range tones	128 - 255
36877	Noise	128 - 255
36878	Volume	0 - 15

Any value less than 128 POKEd into the first 4 registers will turn them off. A value of 0 turns off the volume. Note that the volume register must contain a non-zero value for the other registers to have any effect. Also, if you are using sound and multicolour graphics simultaneously you must use a mask to protect the bits of 36878 which control multicolour mode.
i.e.   POKE 36878, (PEEK (36878) AND 240) OR VOL
ANDing 240 leaves the multicolour control bits unchanged while forcing the volume control bits to 0. ORing the volume value leaves the top 4 bits unchanged (as long as the value is less than 16) and puts the volume value into the last 4 bits.

Tone Registers

Each tone register covers 3 octaves. However they overlap so that the total range covered is 5 octaves. The following table gives POKE values, frequencies and approximate musical notes for these 3 registers. The values not mentioned produce frequencies somewhere between 2 notes.

Value	High (Hz)	Mid (Hz)	Low (Hz)	Note
128	125.8	62.9	31.5	B
135	133.2	66.6	33.3	C
143	142.7	71.3	35.7	C#
147	148	74	37	D
151	153.7	76.8	38.4	D#
159	166.5	83.2	41.6	E
163	173.7	86.8	43.4	F
167	181.6	90.8	45.4	F#
175	199.8	99.9	49.9	G

Value	High (Hz)	Mid (Hz)	Low (Hz)	Note
179	210.3	105.1	52.6	G#
183	221.9	111	55.5	A
187	235	117.5	58.8	A#
191	249.7	124.8	62.4	B
199	285.4	142.7	71.3	C#
201	295.9	148	74	D
203	307.3	153.7	76.8	D#
207	332.9	166.5	83.2	E
209	347.4	173.7	86.8	F
212	371.6	185.8	92.9	F#
215	399.5	199.8	99.9	G
217	420.5	210.3	105.1	G#
219	443.9	221.9	111	A
221	470	235	117.5	A#
223	499.4	249.7	124.8	B
225	532.7	266.3	133.2	C
227	570.7	285.4	142.7	C#
228	591.9	295.9	148	D
229	614.6	307.3	153.7	D#
231	665.8	332.9	166.5	E
232	694.8	347.4	173.7	F
233	726.4	371.6	185.8	F#
235	799	399.5	199.8	G
236	841.1	420.5	210.3	G#
237	887.8	443.9	221.9	A
238	940	470	235	A#
239	998.8	499.4	249.7	B
240	1065.3	532.7	266.3	C
241	1141.4	570.7	285.4	C#
247	1997.5	998.8	499.4	B
248	2282.9	1141.4	570.4	C#
251	3995	1997.5	998.8	B
253	7990	3995	1197.5	B
254	15980	7990	3995	B

The length of notes can be controlled by a delay loop.

```
e.g.   10 POKE 36875, 217
       20 POKE 36878, 15
       30 FOR J = 0 TO 100 : NEXT
       40 POKE 36875, 0
```

Attack and Decay of notes

These can be thought of as the time it takes for a tone or note to reach peak volume (attack) and the time it takes to drop from peak back to zero volume (decay). Attack and decay determine the type of wave produced i.e. square wave - rise straight to peak, sustain the note and then cut it off straight down.

saw tooth - rise straight to peak and then a gradual decay.

triangular - rise gradually and decay gradually.

If you hold a note at a particular volume level this is called sustaining the note.

Altering the volume level alters the volume for all the registers so all tones you produce from the registers are affected by the volume at the same time.

Attack and decay of notes can be controlled using a loop in which the volume is gradually changed.

```
e.g.  10 POKE 36875, 217
      15 REM Attack
      20 FOR J = 0 TO 15 STEP 0.5 : POKE 36878 , J : NEXT
      25 REM Sustain
      30 FOR J = 0 TO 100 : NEXT
      35 REM Decay
      40 FOR J = 15 TO 0 STEP −1 : POKE 36878 , J : NEXT
```

Of course you cannot change the characteristics of the 3 diferent notes independently.

Notes can be made to waver by changing the volume during the sustain period.

```
e.g.  10 POKE 36875, 207 : POKE 36874, 207
      20 FOR J = 0 TO 100
      30 FOR K = 15 TO 5 STEP −1 : POKE 36878, K : NEXT
      40 FOR K = 5 TO 15 : POKE 36878, K : NEXT
      50 NEXT J
```

The VIC 20 can be converted into an electronic organ by assigning note values to the keys. Only 1 octave is covered in the following program, but this could easily be extended.

```
e.g.   10 GET K$ : IF K$ = "" THEN 10
       20 IF K$ = "A" THEN K = 255 : GOTO 140
       30 IF K$ = "S" THEN K = 227 : GOTO 140
       40 IF K$ = "D" THEN K = 228 : GOTO 140
       50 IF K$ = "F" THEN K = 229 : GOTO 140
       60 IF K$ = "G" THEN K = 231 : GOTO 140
       70 IF K$ = "H" THEN K = 232 : GOTO 140
       80 IF K$ = "J" THEN K = 233 : GOTO 140
       90 IF K$ = "K" THEN K = 235 : GOTO 140
      100 IF K$ = "L" THEN K = 236 : GOTO 140
      110 IF K$ = "Z" THEN K = 237 : GOTO 140
      120 IF K$ = "X" THEN K = 238 : GOTO 140
      130 IF K$ = "C" THEN K = 239
```

```
140 POKE 36874, K : POKE 36875, K : POKE 36878, 10
150 FOR J = 0 TO 50 : NEXT
160 POKE 36878, 0
170 K = 0 : GOTO 10
```

Saving and Loading Music

Tone values, volumes and delays can be stored in DATA statements and READ by the program.

```
e.g.   10  FOR K = 0 TO 19
       20  READ M%, V%, D%
       30  POKE 36875, M% : POKE 36874, M% : POKE 36878, V%
       40  FOR J = 0 TO D% : NEXT
       50  POKE 36878, 0 : NEXT K
       60  DATA 236, 10, 50, 247, 15, 100
       70  DATA 131, 7, 30, 221, 7, 50
       50  DATA ... ... ... ...
```

In this case the music will be saved when you save the program.

Alternatively, you can save music in data files on tape or disc. To do this you might first put the values in an array, or DATA statements, and PRINT# them from there to the device.

```
e.g.   Storing a music array on tape:
       10  OPEN 1, 1, 1, "NAME"
       20  FOR J = 0 TO 99
       30  PRINT# 1, M% (J) : NEXT
       40  PRINT# : CLOSE 1

       To read the music from tape into an array:
       10  OPEN 1, 1, 0, "NAME"
       20  DIM M% (99)
       30  FOR J = 0 TO 99
       40  INPUT# 1, M% (J) : NEXT
       50  CLOSE 1
```

You could PRINT# or INPUT# the notes one at a time of course. But, at least for INPUT#, the delay would probably be prohibitive as the buffer once empty would require refilling. If you are using less than a buffer full everything is okay.

Noise Register

This is generally used for special sound effects. Most games are far more engrossing when sound effects are added. (Try watching a suspense film with the volume turned off.) Also, it is generally easier to use a game with sound effects, since they help inform the user what is happening. For example, it is good for the user to hear a shot when the fire key is depressed, or an explosion when something is hit.

CHAPTER 6

EXTERNAL DEVICES

The VIC 20 system can be upgraded with the addition of external devices (peripherals). In this chapter we will describe the more common of these devices - the Datasette, floppy disk drives and printers.

DATASETTE

This is the most economical method of data storage. Its disadvantages, in comparison to disk drives, are that it is relatively slow and can only store program and data files sequentially. So, to access a file that has been passed on the tape, you must manually rewind it. It is a good idea to keep a record of the locations of programs with the tape counter so that they can be quickly located. For the same reason it is best to use short tapes. Even fast forward takes a lot of time to run through a 90 minute tape.

Unlike most microcomputer systems the VIC 20 requires a particular cassette recorder, the Datasette. This has circuitry which enables the VIC 20 to sense whether certain keys are depressed. It can therefore prompt the user when the required key is not pressed. Unfortunately it cannot discriminate between record and play modes. This means that it is still possible to inadvertently write over programs you had meant to read.

Write-protecting tapes

On the near edge of cassettes you will find two write-protect tabs, one for each side of the tape. Breaking these out will lock out the RECORD key, so you will be unable to write onto that side of the tape. Use this method to protect programs with which you do not want to run the risk of overwriting. You can reverse the write-protect by placing a piece of tape over the write-protect opening.

Care of tapes

Avoid touching the tape surface. The oils on your skin can destroy the oxide coating, thus corrupting your data. Store cassettes away from magnetic fields, which can also corrupt data. Television sets produce quite a strong magnetic field, so don't store tapes on or near them.

Relevant BASIC commands
SAVE, LOAD, GET#, INPUT#, OPEN, CLOSE

FLOPPY DISK DRIVES

The VIC 20 can use any of the Commodore disk drives, but the model 1540 is designed to connect directly to the VIC 20. Other models may need an interface cartridge.

Disk drives are more flexible and provide faster access than the Datasette. They can store and access data randomly on any part of the diskette surface. Their disadvantage is that, being precise electro-mechanical devices, they are expensive.

Diskettes come in a protective jacket. Under no circumstances should the diskette be removed from this jacket.

Data storage on diskette

Each diskette used by the 1540 consists of 35 concentric circles called tracks. Each track is broken up into sectors, each of which holds 256 bytes.

Tracks 1-17 have 21 sectors/track
Tracks 18-24 have 19 sectors/track
Tracks 25-30 have 18 sectors/track
Tracks 31-35 have 17 sectors/track

Thus 1 1540 diskette can hold 174,848 bytes (170.75K)

Types of diskette

If you rotate the diskette within its jacket you will find one or more holes which align with the small hole in the jacket. If there is only one hole, the diskette is soft-sectored. If there is more than one hole, the diskette is hard-sectored. The 1540 drive uses only soft-sectored diskettes.

Loading and Unloading Diskettes

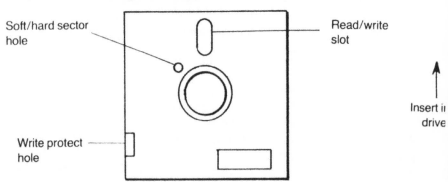

To load a diskette, gently slide it, in the orientation shown above, into the drive slot until it clicks in. Close the slot door. The drive will not operate with the door open.

To unload, press the slot door down and release. The door will open and the diskette will be ejected an inch or so. Remove it carefully.

There are two indicator lights on the drive. The green one is a power-on indicator. The red one lights only when there is some disk activity.

Formatting Diskettes

Before use, a new diskette must be formatted. This writes a disk name, ID number and track and sector information onto the diskette. Formatting is done by the commands:

```
OPEN 1, 8, 15
PRINT#1, "NEW : diskname, ID"
```

The diskname can be any string up to 16 characters long. The ID number should be different for every diskette.

A shorter version of the format command used on diskettes which have previously been formatted will erase all data on the diskette and rename it, leaving the ID number unchanged.

```
OPEN 1, 8, 15
PRINT#1, "NEW : diskname"
```
Note: NEW may be abbreviated to N

Block Availability Map (BAM) and Initialization

The BAM is found on track 18. It contains memory allocation information used when the disk drive is accessed. Each time this happens, the drive compares the ID number on the diskette with the ID number held in drive memory. If they don't match, the drive loads the diskette BAM into drive memory and uses this copy to access the diskette. This copying is called initialization. If the ID numbers match, initialization is not carried out. This is why different diskettes should be given different ID numbers. If they're not, the situation could arise where the BAM for another diskette with the same ID number is used to access a diskette. At best this will cause searches to be unsuccessful. At worst programs will be overwritten.

However, if you have given diskettes the same ID numbers, you can force the drive to copy the BAM using the following:

```
OPEN 1,8,15
PRINT#1 "INITIALIZE"
```
This can be abbreviated to:
```
OPEN 1,8,15,"I"
```

Diskette Directory

This is located on track 18. It contains the names, starting sector addresses and file types of all files on the diskette. It can be displayed using the following commands

```
LOAD "$",8
LIST
```

Write-protecting Diskettes

Like cassette tapes, diskettes can be write-protected. This is done by covering the write-protect slot on the edge of the diskette jacket with tape. Removing the tape restores the diskette to read/write condition.

File Manipulation Commands

Renaming files.
This is done with the commands:
```
OPEN 1,8,15
PRINT#1,"RENAME : NEW—NAME=OLD—NAME"
```
R is an acceptable abbreviation for RENAME

Erasing files

This is done with the commands:

    OPEN 1,8,15
    PRINT# 1, "SCRATCH : FILENAME"
    S is an acceptable abbreviation for SCRATCH

Copying files

This is done with the commands:

    OPEN 1,8,15
    PRINT# 1,"COPY : NEW—NAME = OLD – NAME"
    C is an acceptable abbreviation for COPY

Joining files

This is done with the commands:

    OPEN 1,8,15
    PRINT# 1,"COPY : NEW—FILE=FILE1,FILE2

Note: Disk command strings must not be greater than 40 characters in length.

Validate

This command does housekeeping on the diskette, deleting any files that were not properly closed, and freeing blocks which may have been allocated as temporary storage but are not now associated with any file.

Multiple Disk Systems

If you have a multiple disk system you may need to assign different device numbers to the different drives. At power-up they are all device number 8. Drives can have device numbers 8, 9, 10 and 11. To change the device number:

1) Turn off all drives but the one you are changing
2) Open a command file to the device
    e.g. OPEN 1, 8, 15
3) Type PRINT# 1, "M-W" CHR$ (119) CHR$ (0) CHR$ (2) CHR$ (new-device-number + 32) CHR$ (new-device-number+64)

Leave that drive on. Turning it off will erase the new device number. Turn on the next drive you want to change. This is now device 8 so you alread have a command channel open to it. If you want to change it or have more drives be sure to use different device number.

Closing Disk Files

When a program writes to, or reads from, a disk, the data is first placed in a buffer. Only when the buffer is full is the data actually written to the diskette or, only when it is empty is more data read in. Thus, if you finish writing to the disk with the buffer not full, this data will not be stored on disk. To avoid this, you must close the file. This automatically writes the buffered data to disk, whether or not the buffer is full.

Maximum Number of Opened Files

The VIC 20 can only handle 10 open files at a time, and only 5 of these to disk. It is therefore a good idea to close all files immediately after use.

Disk Data Files

Three types of file can be stored on disk. Program files have already been dealt with. The other two are sequential and random access files.

Sequential Files

These must first be opened using the following format:
OPEN lf , dev , sa , "dn : filename , SEQ , W"

lf	-	logical file number
dev	-	device number
sa	-	secondary address
dn	-	drive number - this may be omitted on single-drive systems
SEQ	-	indicates sequential file
W	-	indicates write mode - it can also be R for read.

e.g. OPEN 1, 8, 4, "0 : RECIPES , SEQ , W"
To overwrite an existing file use an "@" before the drive number.
e.g. OPEN 1, 8, 4, "@0 : RECIPES , SEQ , W"
This also applies to program files.
e.g. SAVE "@0 : PROG-NAME" , 8

Random Access files

These are created by directly addressing diskette sectors and memory buffers. There are 8 buffers available on the VIC 20 but 4 of these are used by the BAM, variable space, command channel I/O and the disk controller, so don't open more than 4 buffers at a time. The format for opening a random access file is as follows:

OPEN lf,dev,sa,"#buff nr"

lf	-	logical file number: 2-14 for data transfer, 15 for utility commands (see below)
dev	-	device number
sa	-	secondary address (2-14)
buff nr	-	buffer number. This can be ommitted as the Disk Operating System (DOS) will automatically select one.

Information is written to random access files using the PRINT# command

Disk Utility Instructions

Block-Read

Purpose	-	reads any sector into one of the memory buffers
To use	-	1) Open a command channel

OPEN 15,8,15
2) Open a direct access channel
e.g.   OPEN 2,8,4,"#"
3) Specify track and sector and read it in.
PRINT#15,"B-R:"sa;dn;T;S
sa - secondary address from 2 above
dn - drive number - mandatory when using direct access commands

You may now use GET# and INPUT# to get the data from the buffer.
e.g. GET#2,B
Check ST for end of data
Close all files when you are through.
Note: B-R is an acceptable abbreviation for BLOCK-READ

Block-Allocate

Purpose	-	checks a sector to see whether it is availabe or already allocated. If available it marks it in the BAM as allocated. If already allocated, it leaves the BAM unchanged and returns the next available track and sector in the error channel. If no sector is available it returns track 0, sector 0, which is non-existent. If the sector you initially asked for is available the message 'OK' is returned in the error channel.
To use	-	1) Open command channel

OPEN 15,8,15
2)   Specify track and sector and check it.
PRINT#15,"B-A":0;T;S
T - Track number
S - Sector number
3)   Check error channel
INPUT#15,E,EM$,T,S
E - error code
EM$ - error message
T - track
S - sector
Proceed on the basis of the error channel return.
4)   Close channels

Note: B-A is an acceptable abbreviation for BLOCK-ALLOCATE

BLOCK-WRITE

Purpose	-	To write data to a sector specified by you. With this instruction you can write to the BAM or the directory, thus destroying them, so it is wise to use a BLOCK-ALLOCATE first, to find a free sector.
To use	-	1) Do a BLOCK-ALLOCATE (not mandatory, but wise)

2)   If EM$='OK' or other free sector returned, continue
3)   Open direct access file
e.g.   OPEN3,8,4,"#"
4)   PRINT# the data - from DATA statements, arrays keyboard
e.g.   PRINT#3,A

5) The data is now in the buffer. To block-write it use:

PRINT#15,"B-W:"4;0;T;S

6) Close files

Note: 1) The format for the BLOCK—WRITE instruction is the same as for BLOCK-READ

2) B—W is an acceptable abbreviation for BLOCK-READ

BUFFER-POINTER

Purpose   -   To change the buffer pointer to start GETting at a particular byte, rather than starting at the first byte in the buffer

To use   -   1) Do a block-read to the point where you are about to GET# bytes

2) Change the buffer pointer

e.g. PRINT#15,"B-P:"sa;byte

sa - secondary address used in setting up the direct access file

byte - number of byte you want to start GETting at

e.g. PRINT#15,"B-P:"4;47

Note: B-P is an acceptable abbreviation for BUFFER-POINTER

BLOCK-FREE

Purpose   -   to de-allocate any block on the disk.

To use   -   1) Open command channel

OPEN15,8,15

2) Specify track and sector and free it

PRINT#15,"B-F:"dr;T;S

dr - drive number

T - track number

S - sector number

e.g. PRINT#15,"B-F:"0;1;4

Note: B-F is an acceptable abbreviation for BLOCK-FREE

Disk Drive Memory Manipulation

The 1540 drive controller contains a 6502 microprocessor. It has 2K of RAM and DOS, which resides on ROM. Some of the RAM is used for housekeeping. The rest is used for buffers. This is also available to the programmer for machine code programs.

The buffers are:

Buffer	Address (hex)
1	300 - 3FF
2	400 - 4FF
3	500 - 5FF
4	600 - 6FF
5	700 - 7FF

Buffer 5 is often used by DOS, so it is not advisable to use it for machine language programs. If you intend to use buffer space for machine code, specify the buffers you want for direct access files, rather than leaving it up to DOS which may overwrite your machine code if left to its own devices.

MEMORY-WRITE

Purpose	-	to store machine code in drive memory
To use	-	a singe M-W commands allows you to store up to 34 bytes
	-	All the data must be transferred as character strings using CHR$
	-	The number of bytes to be stored must be indicated
	-	ONLY the abbreviation M—W can be used. MEMORY—WRITE, in full, is unacceptable
	-	The machine code must end with an RTS instruction. Otherwise the 1540 may loop endlessly, or do something catastrophic to the data on the diskette.

1) Open command channel and transfer data
   OPEN 15, 8, 15
   PRINT# 15, "M-W" CHR$ (LO-ADDRESS-BYTE) CHR$ (HI-ADDRESS-BYTE) CHR$ (NR-BYTES-TRANSFERRED) CHR$ (BYTE-1) CHR$ (BYTE-2)...
   CLOSE 15

MEMORY-READ

Purpose	-	to read data from drive memory one byte at a time
To use	-	the byte read is transferred through the error channel so use

GET #15 to get it
- ONLY the abbreviation M-R is acceptable. MEMORY-READ, in full, is not
- The address to be read is specified using CHR$, as for MEMORY-WRITE
1) Open command channel
   OPEN15,8,15
2) Specify address and read
   PRINT#15,"M-R"CHR$(LO-ADDRESS-BYTE)CHR$(HI-ADDRESS-BYTE)
   GET#15,A$
   PRINTA$
   CLOSE 15

MEMORY-EXECUTE

Purpose	-	to run a machine language program loaded into drive memory by MEMORY-WRITE

| To use | - | ONLY the abbreviation M-E is acceptable
1) Open command channel
OPEN 15,8,15
2) Specify start address of routine and execute
PRINT#15,"M-E"CHR$(LO-ADDRESS-
BYTE)CHR$(HI-ADDRESS-BYTE)
3) Close channel
CLOSE 15 |

User Commands

U1

| Purpose | - | similar to B-R. The only difference is that U1 reads the 2 bytes preceding the data in the sector. These bytes are the link address to the next sector in the file, giving track and sector. |
| To use | - | same as B-R, but replace B-R with U1. |

U2

| Purpose | - | similar to B-W. The difference is that B-W terminates the file at the sector written. U2 allows you to write the link address, ie. track and sector - to the next sector in the file |
| To use | - | same as B-W but replace B-W with U2 |

U3-U9

| Purpose | - | similar to M-E but they cause a jump to specific locations as given below: |

U3	$0500
U4	$0503
U5	$0506
U6	$0509
U7	$050C
U8	$050F
U9	$FFFA

These locations are only 3 bytes long as they are intended to hold a JMP instruction to a location the programmer defines.

U (or UJ)

| Purpose | - | jumps the DOS to its power-up routine |
| To use | - | all the U3-J commands have the following syntax for use:
OPEN 15,8,15
PRINT#15,"U4"
CLOSE15 |

The 1515 Graphic Printer

This has a built in character set including upper and lower case letters, numbers and graphics. To access the printer you must first open a file to it using the following syntax:

OPEN lf,dev,sa

lf	-	logical file number (0-255)
dev	-	device number - either 4 or 5 - it is selected using a switch at the rear of the printer
sa	-	used to select between character sets. If omitted the default character set (upper case & graphics) is used. If sa = 7 the alternate character set (lower case) is selected.

Semicolon

This has the same effect as it does on a screen display

TAB and SPC

These cannot appear immediately after a PRINT#
ie. PRINT#1,TAB(6) is illegal; PRINT#1,"";TAB(6) is OK
On the printer, both TAB and SPC have the same effect as SPC does on the screen display

POS

This reproduces the screen TAB function on the printer. That is, it starts printing at an absolute position rather than relative to where the current printing is being done.

POS is sent to the printer as CHR$(16). The two characters immediately following this determine the print position.

e.g. PRINT#1,CHR$(16);"16";"starts printing at column 16"

Printer Graphics

The printer has several modes, in which characters received are treated differently. The modes and commands to get into them are shown below:

Mode	Command
Double-width characters	CHR$ (14)
Single-width characters	CHR$ (15)
Reverse characters	CHR$ (18) or "[CTRL] [RVS ON]"
Normal characters	CHR$ (146) or "[CTRL] [RVS OFF]"
Graphics	CHR$ (8)
Alternate character set	CHR$ (17)
Standard character set	CHR$ (143)
Repeat Graphics	CHR$ (26)

These are used in PRINT# statements
e.g. PRINT#1,CHR$(17);"LOWER CASE"
Apart from the following two, the functions of the modes are obvious

GRAPHICS mode

This is similar to defining custom character sets in character memory in that it creates patterns of dots. However, in printer graphics, rows not columns are given values, as below, and columns, not rows, are added.

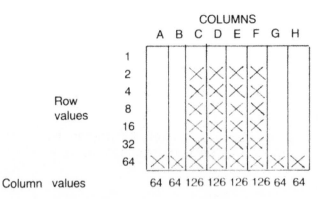

COLUMNS

A B C D E F G H

Row values: 1 2 4 8 16 32 64

Column values: 64 64 126 126 126 126 64 64

Note that only 7 rows are used.
To print this character do the following:

    OPEN# 1 , 4 - open a channel to the printer
    PRINT# 1 , CHR$ (8) - get into graphics mode
    PRINT# 1 , CHR$ (64 + 128) ; CHR$ (64 + 128) ; CHR$ (126 +
    128) ; CHR$ (126 + 128) ; CHR$ (126 + 128) ; CHR$ (126 + 128) ;
    CHR$ (64 + 128) ; CHR$ (64 + 128)

Note that the column values are added to 128. It would of course have
been simpler to put the column values in a DATA statement and read and
PRINT#ed them in a loop.

Repeat Graphics Mode
This mode allows you to repeat a pattern of seven vertical dots up to 255
times per command.
e.g. OPEN 1,4 - open a channel to the printer
    PRINT# 1 , CHR$ (26) CHR$ (5) CHR$ (255)
the first CHR$ value puts the printer into repeat graphics mode. The
second CHR$ value sets the number of repeat(s). The third CHR$ value
defines the vertical dot pattern (in this case just a solid bar 7 dots high)
These two lines will just cause 5 bars to be printed. There is no space
between them, they're continuous.

81

CHAPTER 7

Games Controls

There are three types of games controls in common use - the keyboard, joysticks and paddles. This section describes these, and how they are used.

Keyboard

This is the most common device for games control. Keys are assigned to various functions, such as move left, move right, fire, etc.

When choosing keys for your games, ensure that they are easily usable. Their position should reflect their function. For example, if you have 4 keys for up, down, left and right, use keys in corresponding positions, as below:

```
                    E | up
      left | S                    F | right
                    X | down
```

The space bar makes a good fire button since it's large and hard to miss. It is annoying to have to repeatedly press and release keys to repeat an action, so you should set all keys so that they automatically repeat when held down. This is done by POKEing 128 into byte 650. POKEing 0 into this byte makes only the cursor control keys repeat automatically.

Checking the keyboard.

GET is the command to use to check the keyboard, as it doesn't echo the character typed in, or stop the program to wait for input. It merely checks the keyboard buffer and continues. If there is no character in the buffer the GET variable is set to 0 or the null string. If there is a character in the buffer it is assigned to the variable and the buffer is cleared. The GET variable should be a string variable, since this will accept almost any keystroke (except STOP, RESTORE, SHIFT, CTRL, < = and the colour control keys). If a numeric variable is used you will only be able to GET numeric characters without causing an error.

Having got the character, the program must decide what to do. This can be done in various ways.
(i)   Repeated IF-THEN-
e.g.   10 GET K$
        20 IF K$ = "S" THEN - : GOTO 70
        30 IF K$ = "E" THEN - : GOTO 70

82

```
40  IF K$ = "X" THEN - : GOTO 70
50  IF K$ = "F" THEN - : GOTO 70
60  IF K$ = " " THEN - : GOTO 70
70
```
The statements after the THEN may carry out the required actions and then branch past the rest of the IF statements. If the actions required are too complex to fit on a line, the program may GOTO or GOSUB a section of code to carry out the actions.

(ii)   ON-GOTO-

If you are using many keys, going through all the IF statements may be too time-consuming. It may be quicker to use some calculation on ASCII values with an ON statement. The disadvantage of this technique is that the ASCII values of the characters you are using may be widely seperated, necessitating complex calculations which take as much time as stepping through the IF statements.

(See also "Clearing the keyboard buffer" in Chapter 3.)

Joystick

This consists of a moveable stick and a fire button. When moved, the stick closes 1 or 2 of 4 switches.

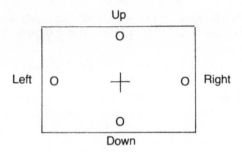

If the stick is moved up or down or to one side, only one switch is closed. If it is moved diagonally, the two switches it moves between are closed.

The state of the switches can be discovered by PEEKing certain memory locations. Each switch controls one bit, delivering a 1 when the switch is closed, a 0 when the switch is open.

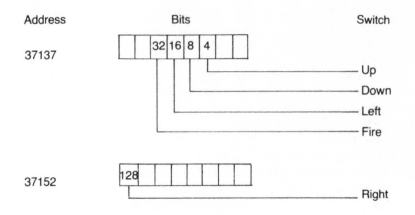

Since the program must check individual bits, bit masks must be used. For example, to check the fire button bit - only use:

FB = (37137) AND 32

Since these locations are used for both input and output, they must be set to input mode before they can be used to read the joystick. This is done by setting the relevant bits of the data direction registers (DDR).

The DDR corresponding to 37137 is located at 37139
The DDR corresponding to 37152 is located at 37154. Location 37139 can simply be POKEd to 0. However, 37154 is also used to control keyboard scanning. So if you wish to use the keyboard, 37154 must be reset to its initial condition after reading the joystick. This is done by the following commands:

```
10  POKE 37154,127 : REM set bit 7 of the DDR to input mode
20  REM read right joystick switch
30  POKE 37154,255 : REM reset bit 7 of DDR to output mode.
```

The following subroutine can be used to read and act on the joystick. Before calling for the first time the DDR controlling 37137 should be set to input mode with POKE 37139,0.

```
9000  REM Joystick control subroutine
9005  POKE 37154,128 : REM Set bit 7 of DDR to input mode
9010  JS=(PEEK(37137) AND 60) + (PEEK(37152) AND 127)
9015  POKE 37154,255 : REM Reset bit 7 of DDR to output mode
9020  ON (JS/4+1) GOTO 9040, 9050, 9060, 9040, 9070, 9080,
      9090, 9040, 9040, 9100
9030  ON (JS-124)/4 GOTO 9110,9120,9130
9040  RETURN : 0 joystick value
9050  Up routine : RETURN
9060  Down routine : RETURN
9070  Left routine : RETURN
9080  Up/left routine : RETURN
9090  Down/left routne : RETURN
```

```
9100   Fire routine : RETURN
9110   Right routine : RETURN
9120   Up/right routine : RETURN
9130   Down/right routine : RETURN
```

Paddles

These consist of a variable resistor ('pot') controlled by a rotating knob, and a fire button. The value of the 'pot' is read by the VIC 20 and converted to a value between 0 and 255. The fire button on one paddle controls the same bit as the left joystick switch, the fire button on the other paddle controls the same bit as the right joystick switch.

Address	Contents
36872	Left pot value
36873	Right pot value
37137	Left fire button (AND with 16)
37152	Right fire button (AND with 128)

Since the right fire button, like the right joystick switch, interferes with the keyboard scanning, the same technique must be used to avoid 'colliding' with the scanner.

CHAPTER 8

HARDWARE

Inside the VIC 20

Although a great deal can be learnt about the VIC 20 without ever taking its cover off, a better understanding of how the machine functions as a computer is obtained by looking at its actual working parts. Don't forget though that this may void your warranty. If you are not worried about this then go ahead and follow all the instructions given below. Providing you do no more than you are instructed nothing can happen to your VIC 20.

In order to take the cover off, first disconnect all the connectors - especially the power connector, and then place the computer keyboard-down on a flat surface.

Along the front edge of the VIC 20 there are three short cross-headed screws that now need to be removed. Then the computer can be turned over and the top of the computer gently lifted. The top is hooked along the rear edge and therefore has to be freed by tipping the whole of the cover backwards. Do this gently so as to not strain the keyboard connector or the connector to the power LED.

If wished, these two connectors may be disconnected. The keyboard connector being freed by gently easing it upwards and the power LED connector by gently easing it backwards. However, there should be sufficient length in the wires so as to allow the top of the computer to rest face-down behind the main body of the VIC 20 without the need to meddle with the connectors.

The parts of the VIC 20 can now be inspected

First look at the keyboard - it is **not** recommended that this be dismantled any further. The springs under the keys can easily be seen and it can be appreciated how these springs result in the characteristic 'clattering' of the keyboard as it is used. The keyboard is joined to the printed circuit board (PCB) by a single 20 channel connector but only 18 of the lines are used. Line 1 (the numbers appear of the PCB along the outer side of the connector) is a GND connection. Line 3 is connected to the RESTORE key. Lines 5-12 are each connected to a separate column of keys on the keyboard and lines 13-20 to a separate row of keys. It is therefore possible to decide using the latter 16 keys just which of the 64 different keys on the keyboard is being pressed.

Next look at the single PCB in the main part of the computer. It may be necessary to lift up a cardboard guard first so as to get a clear view of the silicon chips and the other items on the PCB. Although looking at the working parts of the VIC 20 can do no harm it is again not recommended that any parts be removed from the PCB - except by a skilled person.

Around the edge of the PCB can be seen the eight connectors that are used to join the main PCB to the following:
In clockwise order from the top lefthand corner -
1.   The user port.
2.   The cassette port.
3.   The serial I/O port.
4.   The audio and video outlet.
5.   The memory expansion port.
6.   The power connection.
7.   The game I/O port.
and on the lefthand side
8.   The keyboard connector.

The more important of the silicon chips that are to be found on the PCB will now be discussed in turn.

Starting on the right there is a parallel pair of chips called UE11 and UE12. These two chips are 64K bit ROMs (8K byte ROMs). UE11 is the BASIC ROM whose start address is $C000 and UE12 is the OPERATING SYSTEM ROM whose start address is $E000.

The next chip along, UE10, is the 6502A microprocessor itself.

The nearest chip to the microprocessor, UD9, is a 13 input NAND gate (a 74133) that allows data to pass through a transceiver on the data bus whenever the microprocessor is required to be in contact with memory for either the reading or writing of data.

The next three chips, UD8, UE8 and UF8 are all octal bus transceivers (74245s).

UD8 is a transceiver for the lower 8 address lines of the address bus and allows the microprocessor to address memory only during 'system phase-2' time.

UE8 is a transceiver for address lines A8 - A12, a line named COLOUR that is high only when the video RAM is being addressed, a line named BLK4 that is high unless block 4 of memory, $8000-$BFFF, is being addressed, and the READ/WRITE line from the microprocessor. Once again the transceiver only allows these lines to be connected when the microprocessor is in true contact with the memory-system phase-2 time.

UF8 is the transceiver for the data bus and only allows the passage of data when the microprocessor is addressing memory that actually exists in the unexpanded VIC 20.

UD7 is a 32K bit ROM. This chip is the character generator and holds the bit pattern of all the characters that may be shown on the screen. The base address of the chip is $8000.

The next ten chips, UD2 - UD6 and UE2-UE6, are the ten 4K bit RAM chips (2114s) that form the 5K of RAM of the unexpanded VIC 20. The 'D' chips are the holder of the lower four data bits of each byte and the 'E' chips the holders of the upper four data bits. UE2 and UE3 have the start address of $0000 and the other eight chips provide RAM from $1000 - $1FFF. Note that a 2114 RAM chip holds 1,024 half bytes of data.

The chip named UE1 is also a 2114 RAM chip and is used as the colour RAM in the VIC 20 system. The base address for this chip is $9400 and the half-way address is $9600. The upper part of this chip is the actual colour RAM of the unexpanded VIC 20 with the lower half being unused. Whereas when there is RAM above $2000 the use of this RAM chip is reversed.

Note that the colour RAM in use is only 512 half bytes.

Associated with the colour RAM chip is the chip named UD1. This chip is a quad bilateral switch (a 4066) that in system phase-2 time connects the four outputs of the colour RAM chip to the lower four lines of the data bus. However in system phase-1 time (the complementary time) it prevents the output from the colour RAM going to the main data bus allowing it to go only onto the special 'video data bus' that goes to the video interface chip (VIC)

All of the chips in row 'C' are gating chips of one kind or another.

UC2 is a simple hex inverter (a 7404) that is used to invert the signal on six separate lines.

UC3 is a quad 2 input NOR chip (a 7402) that is used for a variety of purposes.

UC4, UC5 and UC6 are all 3-8 line multiplexers (74138s) that are used as address decoders.

UC4 uses as its three input lines, the address lines A10, A11 and A12 and as as its chip select lines, address line A13 and BLK0 (active when a location in the first 8,192 locations of memory is being addressed). The result of these conditions is that this chip has the effect of decoding the first 8K of memory into eight 1K blocks. The output signals produced are then used as chip select lines for the appropriate RAM chips.

UC5 uses as its three input lines, the three highest address lines and has as its chip select line, the system phase-2 line. The result is that this chip decodes the complete 64K of possible memory into eight 8K blocks - producing lines BLK0, BLK1, ..., BLK7.

UC6 uses as its three input lines, the three address lines A10, A11 and A12 and has three chip select lines. A15, which is to be at logic '1' and A14 and A13 which are to be at logic '0'. These conditions result in the chip decoding the addresses of the 8K memory starting at $8000 into eight 1K blocks, thereby creating a VIA select line, a video RAM select line + COLOUR, and lines for the spare RAM from $9800 to $9FFF which are designated for I/O chips.

Next to be reached are the two large verstaile interface adapter chips - VIA-1 and VIA-2. These chips are UAB3 and UAB1 respectively.

Next to the VIAs is chip UB4 which is another hex inverter (a 7406) that is mainly used in association with the serial port.

The rather insignificant chip UB6 is the timer for the power-up circuitry. This chip (a 555) pulls the RES or restart line low whenever the power is first connected to the board and hence leads the microprocessor to restart its program.

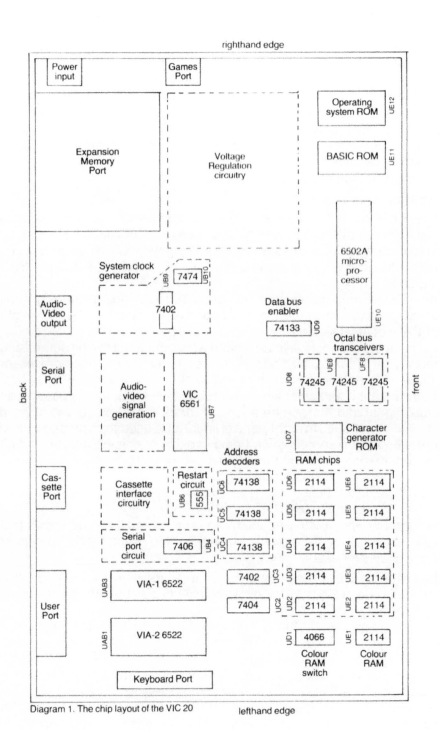

Diagram 1. The chip layout of the VIC 20

UB7 is the important video interface chip - the VIC, coded as a 6561 on the U.K. model VIC 20. This chip produces both the audio and the video output for the VIC 20.

To the right of the VIC are two more chips, UB9 and UB10. The former is a quad 2 input NOR chip and the latter a dual D-type flip-flop.

The block of circuitry between the VIA-1 and the VIC is concerned with the cassette interface. The block behind the VIC is concerned with the audio and video output; the block to the right of the VIC is the system clock generating circuitry; and the block to the right of this is the voltage regulation circuitry.

Diagram 1 shows the chip layout of the VIC 20.

The Microprocessor

At the heart of the VIC 20 is a 6502A microprocessor. This silicon chip is manufactured by MOS TECHNOLOGY and has proved to be one of the most successful microprocessors ever designed. As well as being used in the VIC 20 it is to be found in the APPLE II, the PET and the BBC machine.

The 6502A microprocessor is described as being an eight bit microprocessor which means that it handles its data in the form of eight parallel electrical signals.

This microprocessor is also described as having a sixteen bit addressing mode. That is to say that addresses generated by the microprocessor consist of 16 parallel electrical signals.

At any instant a particular line (=wire) can be considered as passing an actual signal and thereby be a logic '1' or as not doing so and being a logic '0'. This results in eight parallel lines, as is used to carry data to and from a 6502A microprocessor, being capable of holding a 'byte' of data that can be represented in three forms.

     a)   In binary - 00000000 to 11111111
     b)   In hex. - 00 to FF
     c)   In decimal - 0 to 255

No matter in whichever form the byte is considered it can be shown that eight parallel lines are capable of carrying 256 distinct messages to or from a microprocessor.

The sixteen parallel lines that are used to address the memory can also individually be at logic '1' or logic '0' and hence can be represented in the same three forms.

     a)   In binary - 0000 0000 0000 0000 to 1111 1111 1111 1111
     b)   In hex. - 0000 to FFFF
     c)   In decimal - 0 to 65535

In each case it can be shown that 16 parallel lines are capable of carrying 65,536 distinct addresses from the microprocessor.

The eight parallel lines that carry data to and from the 6502A microprocessor collectively form the 'data bus' and the sixteen lines that carry addresses form the 'address bus'.

Diagram 2 shows an elementary representation of how the microprocessor is joined to the memory of the microcomputer.

uni-directional address bus - 16 lines

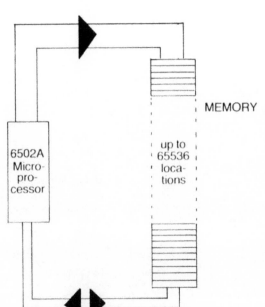

bi-directional data bus - 8 lines

Diagram 2. The microprocessor and the 'memory'.

When a byte of data has to be 'fetched' from a location in memory the address of the required location has first to be placed on the address bus. Then the single byte of data in that location is copied on to the data bus from where it can be read into the microprocessor.

The opposite procedure is followed whenever a byte of data has to be 'stored' in a location in memory. That is to say that the address of the location is placed on the address bus and then the byte of data is copied from a register within the microprocessor and placed on the data bus. The data is then copied into the addressed-location.

A microcomputer system is nominally able to handle a memory with 65,536 locations if it is using a 6502A microprocessor; however, to provide that much memory would make a system rather expensive. The table on the next page shows that actual memory map of the unexpanded VIC 20 and it can be seen from this map that only 26,672 location actually exist. It is usual to describe the size of memory using the term 'K' which denotes 1,024 locations. The memory map therefore shows that an unexpanded VIC 20 uses a little over 26K out of the possible 64K of memory.

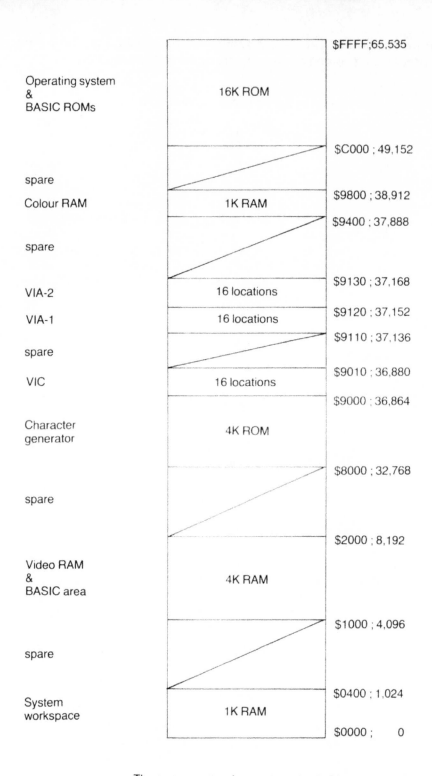

The memory map of an unexpanded VIC20

The fetching of data from memory and the storing of data in memory are two tasks undertaken by the 6502A microprocessor of the VIC 20 but it is the ability of the microprocessor to follow a stored, sequential program that gives the overall system its computing power.

A program for a microprocessor is a carefully ordered collection of bytes of data in memory. Certain of the bytes, the programmer determines, should be viewed by the microprocessor as machine code instructions and certain other bytes as dependant data. The '6502 machine code language' has 151 different machine code instructions, each with its own individual numeric value.

It is important to appreciate that machine code instructions are single bytes of data and therefore each instruction has a value in the range 0 - 255 decimal, 00 - FF hex. or 00000000 - 11111111 binary. Each instruction will occupy a single location in memory and may be transferred to the microprocessor in a single 'fetch' operation.

The microprocessor executes a machine code program in the following manner:

i.   An address register inside the microprocessor, the 'program counter', is made to point to the first instruction of the program.

ii.   The byte of data in the addressed-location, the machine code instruction, is copied into the 'instruction register' of the microprocessor.

iii. The value of the 'program counter' is increased by one so as to point to the following location in memory.
      Note: Steps ii and iii consitute the 'fetch' operation.

iv.   The 'control unit' of the microprocessor then executes the instruction that is in the 'instruction register'. In so doing it may be necessary to 'fetch' bytes of data from the memory.
      Note : Step iv performs the 'execute' operation.

v.   Steps ii-iv are now repeated thereby allowing 'fetch' and 'execute' operations to be performed over and over again.

Diagram 3 shows the nine most important functional parts of the 6502A microprocessor their relationships to the data bus and the address bus.

Each of these functional parts will now be discussed in turn:

The Control Unit.
All of the ordering and the timing of the work performed by the microprocessor is organized by the 'control unit'. In doing its work however it does no more than follow a set of micro-instructions that have been programmed into it by the manufacturer.

The 6502A microprocessor does not have a 'master clock' but is required to have an external device giving it a suitable clock pulse. In the VIC20 system the external clock pulse comes from the Video Interface Chip

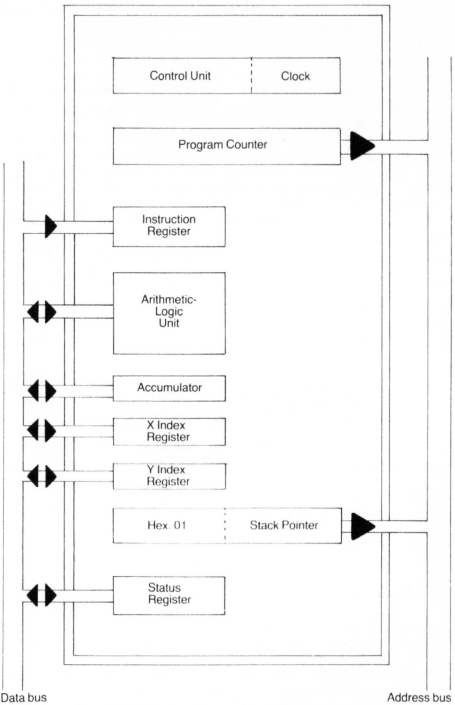

The 6502A microprocessor

Control Unit | Clock

Program Counter

Instruction Register

Arithmetic-Logic Unit

Accumulator

X Index Register

Y Index Register

Hex. 01 | Stack Pointer

Status Register

Data bus

Address bus

Diagram 3. The functional parts of the 6502A microprocessor.

(VIC) which in turn gets its clock pulse from the system clock.

The 'clock' part of the 'control unit' is used to generate timing signals for use within the microprocessor itself as well as the generation of a clock – out pulse on line 39, from which is developed the 'system phase 1 clock pulse' and the complementary 'system phase 2 clock pulse'.

The Program Counter.

As was mentioned above this is an addressing register that is used to point to each location in turn of the machine code program that is being followed by the microprocessor. It is incremented as the last step of the 'fetch' operation.

The Instruction Register.

Again as previously mentioned, this register is used to hold the current instruction that is being executed.

The Arithmetic-logic Unit.

The arithmetic operations of addition and subtraction, together with the logical operations of AND, OR & EOR (exclusive-or), are performed by this part of the microprocessor.

The Accumulator.

This is an eight bit work-register and is the main location for holding numeric data. There are many machine code instructions in the 6502 instruction set that enable the programmer to use this register.

The X Index Register.

This is the second of the work-registers of the 6502A microprocessor and once again there are a large number of machine code instructions that allow the use of this register.

The Y Index Register.

This is the third and final work-register of the 6502A microprocessor.

The Stack Pointer.

This is an eight bit register that holds the low byte of the current address of the 'stack'. On all 6502 systems the area of memory from $01FF down to $0100 (decimal 511 to 256) is used as a 'last-in first-out' workspace for the microprocesor. As the high byte of the address has always to be hex. 01 it has not been necessary for the manufacturer to provide a 16 bit address register as would normally be required.

The Status Register.

This register is a collection of eight flags that have been grouped together to form a register so that they can be preserved, or restored, by copying them to, or from, the stack as determined by the programmer.

The 6502A microprocessor is a 40 pin silicon chip and in the VIC20 system the pins are connected as follows:

Pins 1 & 21: Ground connections.

Pin 2: The RDY or Ready connection is always held at 5V as it is not required.

Pin 3: This clock phase 1 pin is not connected.

Pin 4: The IRQ or Interrupt Request line is joined to the IRQ output of the VIA-2 and is used mainly to generate the 60 interrupts a second for scanning the keyboard.

Pin 5: Not connected.

Pin 6: The NMI or Non-Maskable Interrupt line is joined to the IRQ output of VIA-1 and is activated when the RESTORE key is pressed on the keyboard.

Pin 7: The SYNC line is not connected.

Pin 8: The power line is connected to a 5V supply.

Pins 9-20, 22-25: These are the 16 connections for the address bus.

Pins 26-33: These are the 8 connections for the data bus.

Pin 34: This is the important READ/WRITE line which is held high, logic '1', when a byte of data is to be read from memory, the 'fetch' operation, and goes low, logic '0', during the 'execute' operation if a byte of data has to be 'written' into a location in memory.

Pin 35: Not connected.

Pin 36: Not connected.

Pin 37: The clock-in line that is driven by the clock-out pulse of the Video Interface Chip (VIC)

Pin 38: The Set Overflow line is always held at 5V as it is not required.

Pin 39: The clock-out line that apart from the lag-time may be considered to be the same as the 'system phase-2 clock pulse'.

Pin 40: The RES or Reset line that when brought low for six cycles leads to the microprocessor executing the machine code program starting with the instruction at the address whose high byte is to be found in location $FFFD and low byte in $FFFC.

Diagram 4 shows these connections of the 6502A microprocessor.

The Video Interface Chip

The Video Interface Chip, or VIC as it is normally called, is the second most important silicon chip in the VIC20 microcomputer. It comes second only to the 6502A microprocessor itself.

The VIC is a specially constructed input-output chip (I/O) that has a large variety of functions but its major function is, as its name suggests, the production of the video output signal.

The VIC appears to the microprocessor, and the user, as an addressable block of RAM of 16 locations, $9000-$900F. Each of these locations can be filled or copied, as applies to any other locations that are actually available, with the actions of the VIC being dependant on the values that are placed in the 16 locations.

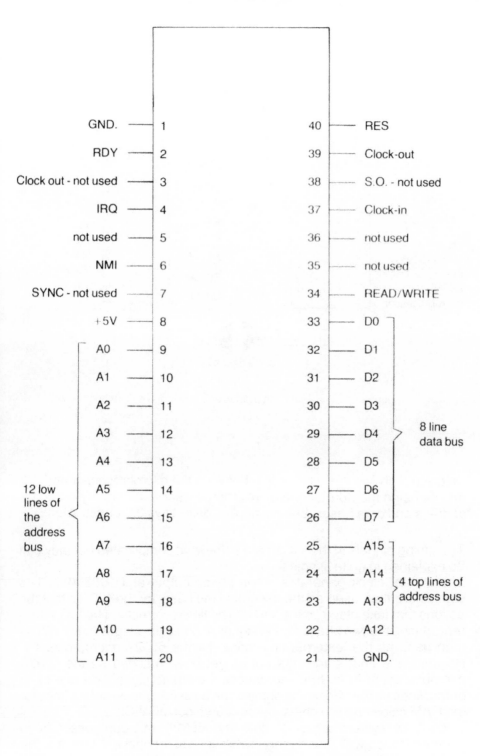

Diagram 4. The 40 lines joining the 6502A microprocessor.

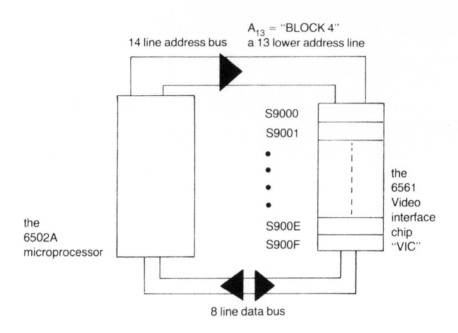

Diagram 5. The relationship between the microprocessor and the VIC.

Diagram 5 shows the relationship between the microprocessor and the VIC as being the normal one of 'microprocessor and memory linked by address and data buses' but this applies only in system phase-2 time.

The timing signals in the VIC20 are somewhat complicated but they can be explained in quite simple terms.

The master clock generates a two phase output at 1.1082 Mhz. The signals are then used as the 'external time base' for the VIC so that the actions that take place on the VIC can be timed correctly. The VIC in turn reproduces the two phase timing signal on one of its output lines which is then used as the 'external time base' for the 6502A microprocessor. However the final stage has not as yet been reached as the 6502A microprocessor in its turn reproduces the timing signals on one of its output lines so that the timing signals can be used as 'chip select' lines for the RAM chips and I/O chips, but of course not the VIC.

Overall, in system phase-2 time the 6502A microprocessor is in communication with its memory, whilst in system phase-1 time it is the VIC that is linked with the memory.

98

Diagram 6 shows the relationship between the VIC and the other parts of the system's memory as occurs in system phase-1 time when the VIC is producing a video output by referring to the colour RAM, the character table and the video RAM.

In the diagram the VIC has been shown as having three separate address buses and three separate data buses in order to explain the principle that three different, complete addresses have to be produced for the different areas of memory, which in turn yield three different items of data. Then the VIC evaluates the data and produces the video output for that character.

These three areas of memory will now be discussed in turn:

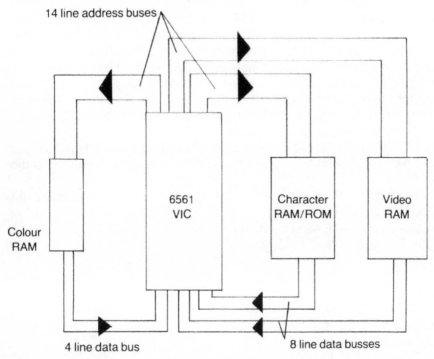

Diagram 6. The relationship between VIC and 'the memory'.

The Video RAM

This is the area of RAM that the user is currently using to hold the ASCII representations of the characters that are to be displayed on the TV screen. In an unexpanded VIC20 the operating system automatically allocates the area of RAM from $1E00-$1FFF for this purpose. However, when extra RAM is added to the system at $2000 it becomes necessary to change the allocation of the video RAM to the area $1000-$11FF. The reason for having to move the video RAM is simply that the 'program area' must be a continuous block of RAM. In the unexpanded system the program area is at $1000-$1DFF, with a standard 3K RAM pack it is at $0400-$1DFF, and with a standard 8K RAM pack it is at $1200-$3FFF.

The VIC20 system uses a display of 22 characters per line and has 23 lines. Therefore the video RAM has to be 506 locations in size. In practice with 512 locations allocated there are always six locations that are unused.

The system variable $0288, decimal 648, is used by the operating system to hold the high byte of the current base address of the video RAM and in an unexpanded VIC20 the line:

PRINT PEEK (648)

gives the answer of '30' which corresponds to the base address $1E00. Interesting effects can be obtained by altering the value of this location!

The colour RAM

In an unexpanded VIC20 the 512 locations in memory from $9600-$97FF are used as the colour RAM, whereas if an 8K expansion RAM is fitted, the block $9400-$95FF is used instead. In either case the locations used are only four bits in size instead of the usual eight bits in size.

The different locations are used to hold the appropriate foreground colour for each character area of the display on the TV screen. There is, therefore, a direct correspondence between the locations of the video RAM, the character table and the colour RAM.

In the VIC20 system there are eight foreground colours and each colour has its own representation for the lower three bits of the locations of the video RAM.

e.g. If the value of the three bits is '000' then the colour for that character area will be 'BLACK'.

The colours and their representations are:

BLACK   000
WHITE   001
RED   010
CYAN   011
PURPLE   100
GREEN   101
BLUE   110
YELLOW   111

The following program shows how the colour RAM can be filled at random with these representations and hence produce a 'quilt' on the TV.

Program: The eight foreground colours

```
10  FOR A=0 TO 505   [For each location]
20  POKE 7680+A,160   [Character 160 — inverse space]
30  POKE 38400+A,RND (1)*8   [A colour at random]
40  NEXT
50  RUN   [Continues forever]
RUN
```

The fourth bit (bit 3) of each location is used to indicate if 'multicolour' is to be used. This is discussed in the graphics chapter.

It is interesting to note that the VIC has a special four line data bus that links the colour RAM to the VIC itself that is used solely to convey the 'colour' data to the VIC.

Diagram 7 shows the actual pin configuration of the VIC. Each line that is attached to the VIC will now be discussed:

Pin 1: Not connected.

Pin 2: The composite colour line of the video output.

Pin 3: The synchronisation and luminance line of the video output.

Pin 4: The video read/write line that is at logic '1' when data is being read from the colour or video RAM.

Pins 5-8: The lines of the special colour data bus.

Pins 9-16: The eight lines of the ordinary data bus.

Pin 17: The input line for 'potentiometer X'.

Pin 18: The input line for 'potentiometer Y'.

Pin 19: The composite sound line of the audio output.

Pin 20: GND.

Pins 21-34: The 14 address lines of the VIC.

Pin 35: The clock-out line that becomes the 'external time base for the 6502A microprocessor.

Pin 36: The system phase-2 clock-out line. Not connected.

Pin 37: Light pen input line.

Pin 38: Clock-in line from the master clock – phase-2 time.

Pin 39: Clock-in line from the master clock – phase-1 time.

Pin 40: +5V.

The internal registers of the VIC:

Each of the registers will now be discussed.

CR0-$9000 – decimal 36864. Usual value decimal 12.

A dual function register.

Function 1: Bit 7 selects interface scan mode for the TV.

Function 2: Bits 0-6 determine the distance from the left hand side of the TV picture to the first column of characters.

   Example: On most modern TV sets the effect of selecting the interface scan mode is to produce a slight rippling on the screen.

Screen shake

This effect can be used to simulate an explosion or collision.

```
10  FOR J = 1 TO 50
20  POKE 36865, 42
30  POKE 36865, 38
40  NEXT
```

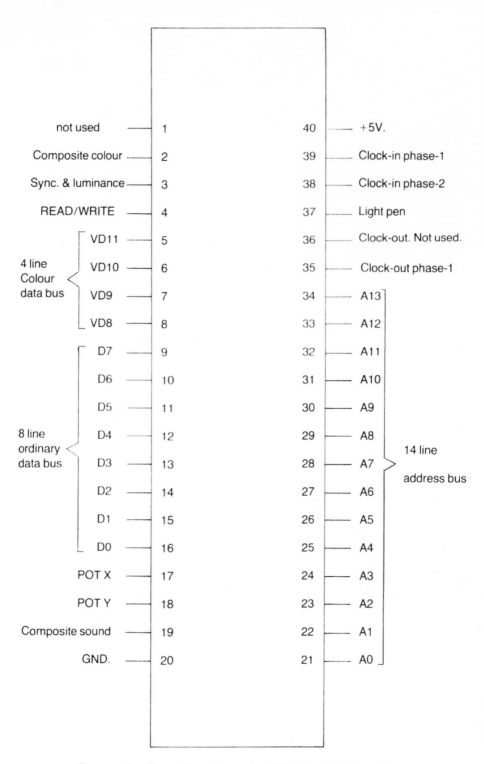

Diagram 7. The 40 lines joining the 6561 Video Interface Chip.

Bit 0 can be set by using the line:

POKE 36864, 140

Program: Positioning the display — horizontally.

This program shows how by changing the value held in $9000 the display can be moved leftwards or rightwards. The cursor direction keys are used to determine the direction required.

```
10 L=0;R=0  [Initialise]
20 IF PEEK(197)=23 AND PEEK(653)=0 THEN R=L
                                      [Cursor right?]
30 IF PEEK(197)=23 AND PEEK(653)=1 THEN L=-1
                                      [Cursor left?]
40 POKE 36864,(PEEK(36864)+L+R) AND 127
                                      [Move display]
50 GOTO 10  [Repeat loop]
```

CR1-$9001 — decimal 36865. Usual value decimal 38.

A single function register.

All the bits of this register are used to determine the distance from the top of the TV picture to the first line of characters.

Program: Positioning the display — vertically.

Once again the cursor direction keys are used to indicate in which direction the user wishes to move the display.

```
10 U=0;D=0  [Initialise]
20 IF PEEK(397)=31 AND PEEK(653)=0 THEN D=1
                                      [Cursor down?]
30 IF PEEK(197)=31 AND PEEK(653)=1 THEN U=-1
                                      [Cursor up?]
40 POKE 36865,(PEEK(36865)+U+D) AND 255
                                      [Move display]
50 GOTO 10   [Repeat loop]
```

CR2-$9002 — decimal 36866. Usual value decimal 150.

A dual function register.

The first seven bits of this register determine the number of columns in the TV display. Normally this will be the expected value of 22.

Bit 7 of this register is used to hold the value for line 9 of the address for the video RAM. On an unexpanded VIC20 as the address of the Video RAM is $1E00 and therefore this bit 7 is set, however when the video RAM is moved to $1000 then bit 7 becomes reset.

CR3-$9003 — decimal 36867. Usual value 174.

A triple function register.

Bit 7 holds the lowest bit of TV raster counter and is therefore alternately set and reset.

Bits 1-6 of this register determine the number of rows in the TV display. The value of these bits will normally be 23.

Bit 0 is very special as it controls whether normal sized characters or double sized characters are to be displayed. The normal size for a character is 8*8 pixels and is selected by bit 0 being reset, however double sized characters, 16*8 pixels, can be selected by having this bit set. The following program shows the effect of setting this bit but still using the normal character table.

Program: Double-size characters

```
10  POKE 36867,PEEK(36867) OR 1   [Set bit 0]
20  FOR A=48 TO 90   [Digits & letters]
30  PRINT CHR$(A);   [Print them out]
40  FOR B=1 TO 700   [Delay]
50  NEXT B,A
60  POKE 36867,PEEK(36867) AND 254
                         [Revert to normal size at end]
```

When this program is run it will be seen that the lower border to the display is lost and that the characters displayed are double sized with one 8*8 character above another.

The facility for being able to use double sized characters is not very useful on an unexpanded VIC20 as there is insufficient RAM to define a reasonable number of double sized characters.

CR4-$9004 — decimal 36868. No usual value.
This register, together with bit 7 of CR3, forms the TV raster counter. On a 625 line TV this register will count between 0 and 255, and the whole counter between 0 and 311.

CR5-$9005 — decimal 36869. Usual value 240.
A dual function register.
Bits 4-7 holds the values of the topmost four address lines for the Video RAM and bits 0-3 the corresponding values for the character table.
Of all these values bits 3 & 7 have a special significance, as whenever this bit is set the memory selected will be in 'block 0', i.e. from $0000-$1FFF, and when reset in 'block 4', i.e. from $8000-$9FFF.
In normal operation of a VIC20 this register holds the value 240 decimal and this leads to the Video RAM being situated at $1E00 and the character table at $8000. These addresses are found as follows:
Video RAM — bit 7 is set, thereby addressing 'block 0'.
— Address lines A12, A11, A10, and A9 are all set and the full address is 'logically' $1E00 as A13, A14, A15 can be considered as reset for 'block 0'.
Character table — bit 3 is reset, thereby addressing 'block 4'.
— Address lines A12, A11 and A10 are all reset and the full address is 'logically' $8000 as A15 can be considered as set and A13 and A14 is reset for 'block 4'.

By altering the values held in CR5 it is possible to move both the Video RAM and the character table. There is not really any advantage in the user being able to move the Video RAM although the following program does give an interesting effect when this is tried.
Program: Moving the Video RAM

```
10  FOR A=128 TO 240 STEP 16   [Eight times]
20  POKE 36869,A   [Move the Video RAM]
30  FOR B=1 TO 500   [Delay]
40  NEXT B,A   [Again]
RUN
```

On the first loop the Video RAM is at $0200 which actually exists, but on the next three loops the address formed is for non-existent RAM at $0600, $0A00 and $0E00. However on the last four loops RAM exists again. The program finishes with the Video RAM being at $1E00 as is normal for an unexpanded VIC20.

On the other hand the facility for moving the character table can be very useful as it enables the user to define his own set of characters. The amount of memory that is required for a full set of 256 characters of size 8*8 is 2K, and of size 8*16 is 4K. However the user does not need to fill all of the locations in the block but only the appropriate ones for the characters that are being used.

The character generator ROM of the VIC20 is a 4K ROM and holds a full set of 'upper case' characters between $8000 and $87FF, and a full set of 'lower case' characters between $8800 and $8FFF. The lower case characters are normally selected by depressing the commodore and shift keys together but they can also be selected by setting bit 1 of the control register, CR5, as is done by the line:
POKE 36869, PEEK (36869) OR 2
The upper set of characters is selected by the line:
POKE 36869, PEEK (36869) AND 253

If it is wished to set up a character table in RAM then this is limited on the standard models to 'block 0' of memory, $0000-$1FFF. In this 8K block of memory it is possible to have eight different starting addresses for the character table although some of the addresses, e.g. $0000 itself, are clearly not available. In every case bit 3 of CR5 must be reset. Bits 0-2 are set then as required to form the appropriate address. The following program shows the effect of selecting the eight possible starting addresses, in turn, on an unexpanded VIC20.

Program: Moving the character table.

```
10 FOR A=248 TO 255   [Eight times]
20 POKE 36869,A  [Move the character table]
30 FOR B=1 TO 500   [Delay]
40 NEXT B,A   [Again]
50 POKE 36869,240   [Revert to the ROM]
RUN   [— upper case]
```

CR6-$9006 — decimal 36870. Usual value 0.
This register is used in conjunction with the light pen and holds the 'horizontal position'.

CR7-$9007 — decimal 36871. Usual value 0.
The 'vertical position' of the light pen.

CR8-$9008 — decimal 36872. Usual value 255.
The counter for potentiometer 1.

CR9-$9009 — decimal 36873. Usual value 255.
The counter for potentiometer-2.

CRA-$900A — decimal 36874. Usual value 0.
This register controls 'speaker-1'. Bit 7 is the on/off control bit, whilst bits 0-6 select the actual note. Speaker-1 has an 'alto voice'.

CRB-$900B — decimal 36875. Usual value 0.
This register controls 'speaker-2', the 'tenor voice'.

CRC-$900C — decimal 36876. Usual value 0.
This register controls 'speaker-3', the 'soprano voice'.

CRD-$900D — decimal 36877. Usual value 0.
This register controls 'speaker-4', the 'noise' speaker.

CRE-$900E — decimal 36878. Usual value 0.
A dual purpose register.
Bits 0-3 form the counter for the volume control of the four speakers. When all the bits are reset the volume control is 'off' and when all the bits are set the volume control is fully 'on'.
Bits 4-7 hold the user's selection of the auxiliary colour which is only used when 'multicolour' is switched on (see Graphics).

CRF-$900F — decimal 36879. Usual value 27.
This is the main colour selecting register of the VIC and has three distinct functions.

Bits 0-2 are used to hold the 'border 0' colour. In the VIC20 there are eight colours that can be border colours and these are:

0 – 000 – Black
1 – 001 – White
2 – 010 – Red
3 – 011 – Cyan
4 – 100 – Purple
5 – 101 – Green
6 – 110 – Blue
7 – 111 – Yellow

These border colours can be selected by putting the required value into the bits 0-2 of control register CRF.

Program: The different 'border colours'.

```
10  PRINT CHR$(147)   [Clear the screen]
20  FOR A=0 TO 7    [Each border colour in turn]
30  POKE 36879,24 AND A    [Keep bits 3 & 4 set but vary]
40  FOR B=1 TO 500   [bits 0-2]
50  NEXT B,A   [Next]
RUN
```

Note how the border varies whilst the central display does not.
Bit 3 is the 'reverse' field control bit. At any time the state of this bit can be changed to 'reverse' the whole display.

The following lines can be used to 'reverse' the display.
POKE 36879, PEEK (36879) OR 8 ; ordinary
POKE 36879, PEEK (36879) AND 247 ; reverse

Bits 4-7 hold the 'background' colour for the display. There are 16 possible background colours and the following table gives the colours together with their codes. Note that these codes are the same for the 'auxiliary' colours as used in the 'multicolour' mode.

0 – 0000 – Black
1 – 0001 – White
2 – 0010 – Red
3 – 0011 – Cyan
4 – 0100 – Purple
5 – 0101 – Green
6 – 0110 – Blue
7 – 0111 – Yellow
8 – 1000 – Orange
9 – 1001 – Light orange
10 – 1010 – Pink
11 – 1011 – Light cyan

12 — 1100 — Light purple
13 — 1101 — Light green
14 — 1110 — Light blue
15 — 1111 — Light yellow

The following program shows how the 'background' colour can be varied by altering the contents of CRF.

Program: The different 'background' colours.

```
10  PRINT CHR$(147)   [Clear the screen]
20  FOR A=0 TO 240 STEP 16   [Each background colour]
30  POKE 36879,11 OR A   [Keep bits 0,1 & 3 set]
40  FOR B=1 TO 500   [but vary bits 4-7]
50  NEXT B, A
RUN
```

CHAPTER 9

Machine Language Programming

The case for machine language

For many applications, particularly real time applications requiring a quick response, such as games, you will find that BASIC programs are too slow to be satisfactory. The reason for this lies in the fact that BASIC programs are interpreted by another program (the interpreter) before the VIC20 executes them. The interpreter works by reading a BASIC statement, translating that into machine language and handing the translation to the machine, which executes it. The interpreter reads the next BASIC statement and continues the cycle. However, the interpreter never keeps any of the translations. No matter how often it has translated a statement, if it reads it again, it must translate it again. So if a program goes through a loop 100 times, every statement in that loop must be translated 100 times. It becomes obvious that most of the time involved in executing a BASIC program is actually spent translating it into a form the machine can execute. It is equally obvious that by cutting out the translation stage you can write programs that will run much faster than equivalent BASIC programs. Hence machine language.

Machine language programs consist of numbers. Some of the numbers are operation codes (opcodes) which make the machine carry out some simple task. Some of the numbers are addresses, and some are just values. Machine language programs are generally written using an assembler, which translates from assembly language to machine language. If you don't have an assembler for the VIC20 and have to carry out its task yourself, don't worry. Since assembly language instructions are almost a 1-1 match with machine language instructions, the task is fairly easy. The advantage of assembly language is that its instructions are abbreviations for what the instruction does, making it easier to read and debug than machine language, while retaining exactly the same structure as the machine language program. The instructions are called mnemonics because they act as a reminder of what they do.

e.g.   DEX stands for DEcrement the X-register

When writing your own machine language programs it is best to start from a high level. Write down in English what it is you want to do. Break it up into tasks. Then approach each task individually, breaking them down further, until each sub-task is a fairly simple operation.

e.g. GAME
    1)   set up move table
    2)   set up characters
    3)   display background
    4)   Main loop - a) check keyboard and act
                        b) move invaders
                        c) check if hit
    5)   Restart game?
Now take each task and break it up.
e.g. 4c) (i)   check position of ship against position of enemy missiles
        (ii) if they're the same, explode, subtract ship
       (iii) check if game is over
Each of these sub-tasks can also be broken up into smaller sub-tasks.
Only when the final subtasks are very simple should you start writing the
program. You should use this technique for a program in any language,
but for a program in machine language it is crucial. It is so easy to get lost
in the details of machine language programs.

Write the program using mnemonics. Translating these into machine
language is the last step.

Inputting, Saving and Loading machine language programs

Having written your program you now need to store it in the
machine. This can be done using BASIC programs which read the
machine language values from DATA statements or directly from the
keyboard, and poke them into memory.

The following example program protects 512 bytes (7168 - 7679) from
BASIC, prompts the user for byte values and POKEs them into memory.
If you don't want to use this block of memory - you may have a custom
character set there - make sure you change lines 10, 20 accordingly.

```
10  POKE 52, 28 : POKE 56, 28 : CLR
20  BYTE = 7168
30  INPUT V : POKE BYTE , V
40  BYTE = BYTE + 1 : GOTO 30
```

To check what you've put in you might use something like the following:

```
10  BYTE = 7168
20  PRINT BYTE ; PEEK (BYTE) ; PEEK (BYTE + 1) ; PEEK
    (BYTE + 2) ; PEEK (BYTE + 3)
30  BYTE = BYTE + 4
40  GET K$ : IF K$ = " " THEN 40
50  IF K$ = " " THEN 20
```

This prints the values of 4 bytes, waits for the space character and prints
the next 4 bytes. Any character other than space will end the program.

110

Saving and loading machine language programs to and from tape or disk can be done by treating them as data files.

e.g. saving to tape

```
10 OPEN 1, 1, 2, "MACHINE"
20 INPUT "FIRST BYTE" ; S
30 INPUT "LAST BYTE" ; L
40 FOR J = S TO L
50 PRINT# 1, PEEK (J) : NEXT
60 PRINT# 1 : CLOSE 1
```

e.g. loading from tape

```
10 POKE 52, 28 : POKE 56, 28 : CLR (or the appropriate values)
20 OPEN 1, 1, 0, "MACHINE"
30 BYTE = 7168 (or the appropriate address)
40 GET# 1, V
50 IF ST = -128 THEN CLOSE 1 : END
60 POKE BYTE, V : BYTE = BYTE + 1 : GOTO 40
```

All of these examples are skeleton programs, just to give you the idea. You should change them by adding features which you find useful.

Writing machine language programs is detailed and can be tedious, since you make all decisions, such as where to store variables, strings and so on. It is therefore advisable to mix BASIC and machine language programs, using BASIC where speed is not essential. For example, most games need some initialization; setting up backgrounds, loading character sets, and so on. You could use BASIC for these tasks and then use a SYS statement to call the machine language program to actually run the game.

Disabling STOP and RESTORE Keys

A handy routine for use with most machine code programs is one to disable the RUN/STOP and RESTORE keys.

To disable the STOP key : POKE 808, 114

To disable the RESTORE and STOP keys : POKE 808, 100

To enable both keys : POKE 808, 112

You should also note that there are useful machine language subroutines in ROM (Kernal routines) which can be used. Their use will save you time and RAM. You will find a list of these in Appendix D.

Programming in 6502 machine language

Any computer consists basically of a processor and memory. The VIC20 uses a 6502 microprocessor. The rest of this chapter deals with the 6502 instruction set and how to use it.

Registers

Almost all calculations are done in the microprocessor. Registers are special pieces of memory in the processor which are used to carry out, and store information about, calculations. The 6502 has the following registers:

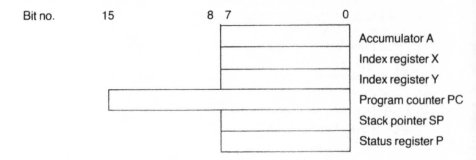

(i) Accumulator A

This is probably the most important register to the user, since most calculations and logical operations are carried out using it.

(ii) Index register X

This can do many of the things the accumulator does, and is also used in indexed addressing.

(iii) Index register Y

This is similar to X but is used a little differently in some addressing modes.

(iv) Program counter PC

This contains the address of the program instruction to be executed next.

(v) Stack pointer SP

The 6502 has the memory block $0100 - $01FF reserved as stack, where it stores information (such as return addresses when subroutines are called). The stack pointer contains the address of the next empty byte in the stack. Since the stack pointer is only 1 byte long it only holds the low byte of the address ; 00 - FF. The high byte, 01, is added automatically.

(vi) Status register P

Bits of this register are altered depending on the result of arithmetic and logical operations. These bits - called status flags - are described below:

Bit No.	7	6	5	4	3	2	1	0
Status register	S	V		B	D	I	Z	C

Bit0 - C - Carry flag: this holds the carry out of the most significant bit in any arithmetic operation. In subraction operations however, this flag is cleared - set to 0 - if a borrow is required, set - to 1 - if no borrow is required. The carry flag is also used in shift and rotate logical operations.

Bit1 - Z - Zero flag: this is set to 1 when any arithmetic or logical operation produces a zero result, and is set to 0 if the result is non-zero.

Bit2 - I: this is an interrupt enable/disable flag. If it is set, interrupts are disabled. If it is cleared, interrupts are enabled.

Bit3 - D: this is the decimal mode status flag. When set, and an Add with Carry or Subtract with Carry instruction is executed, the source values are treated as valid BCD numbers. The result generated is also a BCD number.

Bit4 - B: this is set when a software interrupt (BRK instruction) is executed.

Bit5 : not used.

Bit6 - V - Overflow flag: when an arithmetic operation produces a result too large to be represented in a byte, V is set.

Bit7 - S - Sign flag: this is set if the result of an operation is negative, cleared if positive.

The most commonly used flags are C, Z, V, S.

Addressing modes

Instructions need operands to work on. There are various ways of indicating where the processor is to get these operands. The different methods used to do this are called addressing modes. The 6502 offers 11 modes, as described below.

1) Immediate
In this mode the operand's value is given in the instruction. In assembly language this is indicated by "#" before the operand.

e.g. LDA# $0A - means "load the accumulator with the hex value 0A"

In machine code different modes are indicated by different codes. So 'LDA' would be translated into different codes depending on the addressing mode. In this mode, it is:

$A9 $0A (hex)
169 10 (decimal)

2 & 3) Absolute and Zero-page Absolute
In these modes the operand's address is given.

e.g. LDA $31F6 (assembly language)
$AD $31F6 (machine code)

If the address is on zero page - i.e. any address where the high byte is 00 - only 1 byte is needed for the address. The processor automatically fills in the 00 high byte.

e.g. LDA $F4
$A5 $F4

Note the different instruction codes for the different modes.
Note also that for 2 byte addresses, the low byte is stored first.

4) Implied
No operand addresses are required for this mode. They are implied by the instruction.

e.g. TAX - transfer accumulator contents to X-register
$AA - (machine code)

5) Accumulator

In this mode the instruction operates on data in the accumulator, so no operands are needed.

e.g.   LSR - logical bit shift right
$4A (machine code)

6 & 7) Indexed and Zero-page indexed

In these modes the address given is added to the value in either the X or Y index register to give the actual address of the operand.

e.g.   LDA $31F6, Y
$D9 $31F6
LDA $31F6, X
$DD $31F6

Note that the different operation codes determine the index register used.

In the zero-page version, you should note that the X and Y registers are not interchangeable. Most instructions which can be used with zero-page indexing do so with X only.

e.g.   LDA $20, X
$B5 $20

Again, remember that for 2 byte addresses the low byte is stored first. So, if you're POKEing in machine code, the instruction above would be POKEd in the order $DD, $F6, $31. If you're using an assembler, just write the address in the normal order.

8) Indirect

This mode applies only to the JMP instruction - JuMP to new location. It is indicated by parentheses around the operand. The operand is the address of the bytes whose value is the new location.

e.g.   JMP ($215F)

Assume the following -	byte	value
	$215F	$2160
	$76	$30

This instruction takes the value of bytes $215F, $2160 and uses that as the address to jump to — i.e. $3076 (remember that addresses are stored with low byte first).

9) Pre-indexed indirect

In this mode a zero-page address is added to the contents of the X-register to give the address of the bytes holding the address of the operand. The indirection is indicated by parentheses in assembly language.

e.g.   LDA ($3E,X)   (assembly language)
$A1 $3E   (machine code)

Assume the following -   byte   value
                            X-register $05
                            $0043 $15
                            $0044 $24
                            $2415 $6E

Then the instruction is executed by:
(i)   adding $3E and $05 = $0043
(ii)   getting address contained in bytes $0043, $0044 = $2415
(iii) loading contents of $2415 - i.e. $6E - into accumulator
Note a) When adding the 1-byte address and the X-register, wrap around
        addition is used - i.e. the sum is always a zero-page address.
        e.g. FF + 2 = 0001 *not* 0101 as you might expect.
      b) Only the X-register is used in this mode.

10) Post-indexed indirect
In this mode the contents of a zero-page address (and the following byte)
give the indirect address, which is added to the contents of the Y-register
to yield the actual address of the operand. Again, in asembly language,
the indirection is indicated by parentheses.
e.g.   LDA ($4C), Y
Note that the parentheses are only around the 2nd byte of the instruction
since is is the part that does the indirection.
Assume the following -   byte   value
                             $004C   00
                             $004D   21
                             Y-register   05
                             $2105   6D
Then the instruction above executes by:
(i)   getting the address in bytes $4C, $4D = $2100
(ii)   adding the contents of the Y-register = $2105
(iii) loading the contents of the byte $2105 - i.e. 6D - into the accumulator
Note: only the Y-register is used in this mode.

11) Relative
This mode is used with Branch-on-Condition instructions. It is probably
the mode you will use most often. A 1 byte value is added to the program
counter, and the program continues execution from that address. The 1
byte number is treated as a signed number - i.e. if bit 7 is 1, the number
given by bits 0-6 is negative; if bit 7 is 0, the number is positive. This
enables a branch displacement of up to 127 bytes in either direction.
e.g. bit no. 7 6 5 4 3 2 1 0   signed value   unsigned value
      value   1 0 1 0 0 1 1 1   -39 $B7
      value   0 0 1 0 0 1 1 1   +39 $27
Instruction example:
      BEQ $B7 (assembly language)
      $F0 $B7 (machine code)

This instruction will check the zero status bit. If it is set, 39(decimal) will be subtracted from the program counter and execution continues from that address. If the zero status bit is not set, execution continues from the following instruction.

Notes: a) The program counter points to the start of the instruction after the branch instruction before the branch displacement is added. Remember to take this into account when calculating the displacement.

e.g. address   instruction
      $6040   BEQ $B7
      $6042   - - - -

Before the branch is carried out the PC will contain $6042. So if the branch is executed, the PC will end up containing $6009 (ie. $6042 − 39). If this subtraction looks wrong remember that $6042 is in hex, 39 in decimal.

b) Branch-on-condition instructions work by checking the relevant status bits in the status register. Make sure that they have been set or unset as you want them. This is often done using a CMP instruction.

e.g. Suppose you are using the value in byte $2046 as a loop counter - subtracting 1 from it each time through the loop. At the end of each turn throught the loop you wish to see whether you should leave the loop or go back to the start of it. The following code will do this

      LDA #0
      CMP $2046 (compare counter with zero)
      BNE $B7 (branch −39 to start of loop if status bit Z=0)

The CMP instruction affects only the values of the status bits.

c) If you find you need to branch further than 127 bytes, use the opposite branch-on-condition instruction and a JMP.

e.g. If the loop in the example above was longer than 127 bytes, you could use the following code at the end of the loop.

      LDA #0
      CMP $2046 (compare counter to 0)
      BEQ $03 (if counter=0, branch past JMP instruction)
      JMP $1542 (if counter < >   0, jump to start of loop)

The following table is a summary, in alphabetical order, of the 6502 instruction set. An explanation of notation used in the table follows.

A	—	Accumulator	[addr]	—	contents of address
X,Y	—	Index registers	[[addr]]	—	contents of contents of
P	—	status register			address (indirection)
SP	—	stack pointer	⌄	—	exclusive OR
addr	—	8 bit (zero-page)	v	—	inclusive OR
		address	^	—	AND
addr 16	—	16 bit (absolute)	C	—	logical complement of C
		address			i.e. if C = 1, C = 0
S,V,B,D,I,Z,C	—	status bits			C = C, C = 1
←	—	data trasnferred in	6,7	—	status bits takes on
		direction of arrow (read			value of bits 6, 7 of
		as 'becomes')			memory byte being
/	—	bit changed			operated on.
—	—	unchanged	1,0	—	status bit set, cleared.

The 6502 Instruction Set

Instruction Mnemonic	Mach Code	Bytes	Operation and effect on Status bits	Addressing mode
ADC			Add memory to accumulator with carry	
data	69	2	A←A + data + C	Immediate
addr	65	2	A←A + [addr] + C	zero-page direct
addr16	6D	3	A←A + [addr16] + C	absolute direct
addr,X	75	2	A←A + [addr + X] + C	zero-page indexed
(addr,X)	61	2	A←A + [[addr + X]] + C	pre-indexed indirect
(addr),Y	71	2	A←A + [[addr + 1, addr] + Y] + C	post-indexed indirect
addr16,X	7D	3	A←A + [addr16 + X] + C	absolute indexed
addr16,Y	79	3	A←A + [addr16 + Y] + C	absolute indexed

S V D I Z C
/ /   / /

AND			'And' memory with accumulator	
data	29	2	A←A∧ data	immediate
addr	25	2	A←A∧ [addr]	zero-page direct
addr16	2D	3	A←A∧ [addr16]	absolute direct
addr,X	35	2	A←A∧ [addr + X]	zero-page indexed
(addr,X)	21	2	A←A∧ [[addr + X]]	pre-indexed indirect
(addr),Y	31	2	A←A∧ [[addr + 1, addr] + Y]	post-indexed indirect
addr16,X	3D	3	A←A∧ [addr16 + X]	absolute indexed
addr16,Y	39	3	A←A∧ [addr16 + Y]	absolute indexed

S V D I Z C
/   /

ASL			Shift left 1 bit through carry	

C←7 6 5 4 3 2 1←0

A	0A	1	Carry flag takes value of	accumulator
addr	06	2	bit 7 of byte operated on.	zero-page direct
addr16	0E	3	Bit 1 takes value 0	absolute direct
addr,X	16	2	Bit 7← Bit 6, Bit 6← Bit 5, etc.	zero-page indexed
addr16,X	1E	3		absolute indexed

S V D I Z C
/   / /

BCC			Branch on Carry clear	
displacement	90	2	PC←PC + displacement	relative

S V D I Z C
— — — — — —

BCS			Branch on carry set	
displ	B0	2	PC←PC + displ.	relative

S V D I Z C
— — — — — —

BEQ			Branch on Z = 1	
displ	F0	2	PC←PC + displ	relative

S V D I Z C
— — — — — —

BIT

'AND' accumulator with memory
Only status bits affected.
Z bit changed according to
result of 'AND'

addr	24	2	A & [addr]	zero-page direct
addr16	2C	3	A & [addr16]	absolute direct

S V D I Z C
7 6   /

BMI

Branch on S = 1 (negative result)

displ	30	2	PC ← PC + displ	relative

S V D I Z C
— — — — — —

BNE

Branch on Z = 0

displ	D0	2	PC ← PC + displ	relative

S V D I Z C
— — — — — —

BPL

Branch on S = 0 (positive result)

displ	10	2	PC ← PC + displ	relative

S V D I Z C
— — — — — —

BRK

Force break

	00	1	PC ← PC + 2	implied

[SP] ← PC (HI)
[SP − 1] ← PC (LO)
[SP − 2] ← P
SP ← SP − 3
PC (HI) ← [FFFF]
PC (LO) ← [FFFE]
B ← 1

S V D I Z C
— — — 1 — —

BVC

Branch on V = 0

displ	50	2	PC ← PC + displ	relative

S V D I Z C
— — — — — —

BVS

Branch on V = 1

displ	70	2	PC ← PC + displ	relative

S V D I Z C
— — — — — —

CLC

Clear carry flag

	18	1	C ← 0	implied

S V D I Z C
— — — — — 0

CLD

Clear decimal mode

	D8	1	S V D I Z C	implied

— — 0 — — —

CLI

	58	1	Clear interrupt disable bit	implied

S V D I Z C
— — — 0 — —

CLV

	B8	1	Clear overflow flag	implied

S V D I Z C
— 0 — — — —

CMP — Compare memory with accumulator

data	C9	2	A — data	immediate
addr	C5	2	A — [addr]	zero-page direct
addr16	CD	3	A — [addr16]	absolute direct
addr,X	D5	2	A — [addr + X]	zero-page indexed
(addr,X)	C1	2	A — [[addr + X]]	pre-indexed indirect
(addr),Y	D1	2	A — [[addr + 1, addr] + Y]	post-indexed indirect
addr16,X	DD	3	A — [addr16 + X]	absolute indexed
addr16,Y	D9	3	A — [addr16 + Y]	absolute indexed

S V D I Z C
/ — — — / /

Only the status bits are effected

CPX — Compare memory with X-register

data	E0	2	X — data	immediate
addr	E4	2	X — [addr]	zero-page direct
addr16	EC	3	X — [addr16]	absolute direct

S V D I Z C
/ — — — / /

CPY — Compare memory with Y-register

data	C0	2	Y — data	immediate
addr	C4	2	Y — [addr]	zero-page direct
addr16	CC	3	Y — [addr16]	absolute direct

S V D I Z C
/ — — — / /

DEC — Decrement memory by 1

addr	C6	2	[addr] ← [addr] — 1	zero-page direct
addr16	CE	3	[addr16] ← [addr16] — 1	absolute direct
addr,X	D6	2	[addr + X] ← [addr + X] — 1	zero-page indexed
addr16,X	DE	3	[addr16 + X] ← [addr16 + X] — 1	absolute indexed

S V D I Z C
/ — — — / —

DEX

	CA	1	Decrement X-register by 1	implied

X ← X — 1

S V D I Z C
/ — — — / —

DEY

	88	1	Decrement Y-register by 1	implied

Y ← Y — 1

S V D I Z C
/ — — — / —

EOR

"Exclusive-or" memory with accumulator

data	49	2	A← A∀ data	immediate
addr	45	2	A← A∀ [addr]	zero-page direct
addr16	4D	3	A← A∀ [addr16]	absolute direct
addr,X	55	2	A← A∀ [addr + X]	zero-page indexed
(addr,X)	41	2	A← A∀ [[addr + X]]	pre-indexed indirect
(addr),Y	51	2	A← A∀ [[addr + 1, addr] + Y]	post-indexed indirect
addr16,X	5D	3	A← A∀ [addr16 + X]	absolute indexed
addr16,Y	59	3	A← A∀ [addr16 + Y]	absolute indexed

S V D I Z C
/ — — — / —

INC

Increment memory by 1

addr	E6	2	[addr]← [addr] + 1	zero-page direct
addr16	EE	3	[addr16]← [addr16] + 1	absolute direct
addr,X	F6	2	[addr + X]← [addr + X] + 1	zero-page indexed
addr16,X	FE	3	[addr16 + X]← [addr16 + X] + 1	absolute indexed

S V D I Z C
/ — — — / —

INX

Increment X-register by 1

	E8	1	X← X + 1	implied

S V D I Z C
/ — — — / —

INY

Increment Y-register by 1

	C8	1	Y← Y + 1	implied

S V D I Z C
/ — — — / —

JMP

Jump to new address

addr16	4C	3	PC← addr16	absolute direct
(addr16)	6C	3	PC← [addr16]	indirect

S V D I Z C
— — — — — —

JSR

Jump to subroutine

addr16	20	3	[SP]← PC (HI)	absolute direct
			[SP-1]← PC (LO)	
			SP = SP - 2	
			PC← addr16	

S V D I Z C
— — — — — —

LDA

Load accumulator with memory

data	A9	2	A← data	immediate
addr	A5	2	A← [addr]	zero-page direct
addr16	AD	3	A← [addr16]	absolute direct
addr,X	B5	2	A← [addr + X]	zero-page indexed
(addr,X)	A1	2	A← [[addr + X]]	pre-indexed indirect
(addr),Y	B1	2	A← [[addr + 1, addr] + Y]	post-indexed indirect
addr16,X	BD	3	A← [addr16 + X]	absolute indexed
addr16,Y	B9	3	A← [addr16 + Y]	absolute indexed

S V D I Z C
/ — — — / —

LDX   Load X-register with memory

data	A2	2	X← data	immediate
addr	A6	2	X← [addr]	zero-page direct
addr16	AE	3	X← [addr16]	absolute direct
addr,Y	B6	2	X← [addr + Y]	zero-page indexed
addr16,Y	BE	3	X← [addr16 + Y]	absolute indexed

```
S  V  D  I  Z  C
/  —  —  —  /  —
```

LDY   Load Y-register with memory

data	A0	2	Y← data	immediate
addr	A4	2	Y← [addr]	zero-page direct
addr16	AC	3	Y← [addr16]	absolute direct
addr,X	B4	2	Y← [addr + X]	zero-page indexed
addr16,X	BC	3	Y← [addr16 + X]	absolute indexed

```
S  V  D  I  Z  C
/  —  —  —  /  —
```

LSR   Shift right one bit

A	4A	1	0 →7 6 5 4 3 2 1 0 →C	accumulator
addr	46	2	Carry flag takes value of	zero-page direct
addr16	4E	3	bit 0 of byte operated on.	absolute direct
addr,X	56	2	Bit 7 takes value 0	zero-page indexed
addr16,X	5E	3	Bit 6← Bit 7, Bit 5← Bit 6, etc.	absolute indexed

```
S  V  D  I  Z  C
0  —  —  —  /  /
```

NOP   No operation

	EA	1	implied

```
S  V  D  I  Z  C
—  —  —  —  —  —
```

ORA   Inclusive - or memory with
                                          accumulator

data	09	2	A←Av data	immediate
addr	05	2	A←Av [addr]	zero-page direct
addr 16	0D	3	A←Av [addr 16]	absolute direct
addr,X	15	2	A←Av [addr + X]	zero-page indexed
(addr,X)	01	2	A←Av [addr + X]]	pre-indexed indirect
(addr),Y	11	2	A←Av [addr+1,addr] + Y]	post-indexed indirect
addr16,X	1D	3	A←Av [addr16 + X]	absolute indexed
addr16,Y	19	3	A←Av [addr16 + X]	absolute indexed

```
S  V  D  I  Z  C
/  —  —  —  /  —
```

PHA   Push accumulator onto stack

	48	1	[SP]←A	implied

SP = SP −1

```
S  V  D  I  Z  C
—  —  —  —  —  —
```

PHP

	08	1	Push status register onto stack	
			[SP] ←P	implied
			SP = SP − 1	

S V D I Z C
— — — — — —

PLA
PLA

	68	1	Pull accumulator from stack	
			A← [SP + 1]	implied
			SP← SP + 1	

S V D I Z C
/ — — — / —

PLP

	28	1	Pull status register from stack	
			P← [SP + 1]	implied
			SP← SP + 1	

S V D I Z C
/ / / / / / (from stack)

ROL

Rotate one bit left

A	2A	1		accumulator
addr	26	2		zero-page direct
addr16	2E	3	Carry takes value of bit 7	absolute direct
addr,X	36	2	Bit 0 takes value of carry	zero-page indexed
addr16,X	3E	3	Bit 7←Bit 6, etc.	absolute indexed

`[ 7 6 5 4 3 2 1 0 ←C ]`

S V D I Z C
/ — — — / /

ROR

Rotate one bit right

A	6A	1		accumulator
addr	66	2		zero-page direct
addr16	6E	3	Bit 7 takes value of carry	absolute direct
addr,X	76	2	Carry takes value of bit 0	zero-page indexed
addr16,X	7E	3	Bit 6←Bit 7, etc.	absolute indexed

`[ C→ 7 6 5 4 3 2 1 0 ]`

S V D I Z C
/ — — — / /

RTI

	40	1	Return from interrupt	
			P← [SP + 1]	implied
			PC(LO)← [SP + 2]	
			PC(HI) ← [SP + 3]	
			SP← SP + 3	
			PC← PC + 1	

S V D I Z C
/ / / / / / (from stack)

RTS

	60	1	Return from subroutine	
			PC(LO)← [SP + 1]	implied
			PC(HI) ← [SP + 2]	
			SP← SP + 2	
			PC← PC + 1	

S V D I Z C
— — — — — —

122

SBC   Subtract memory from
                            accumulator with borrow

data	E9	2	A ← A − data − $\bar{C}$	immediate
addr	E5	2	A ← A − [addr] − $\bar{C}$	zero-page direct
addr16	ED	3	A ← A − [addr16] − $\bar{C}$	absolute direct
addr,X	F5	2	A ← A − [addr + X] − $\bar{C}$	zero-page indexed
(addr,X)	E1	2	A ← A − [[addr + X]] − $\bar{C}$	pre-indexed indirect
(addr),Y	F1	2	A ← A − [[addr+1,addr] +Y] − $\bar{C}$ post-indexed indirect	addr16,X
FD	3		A ← A − [addr16 + X] − $\bar{C}$	absolute indirect
addr,Y	F9	3	A ← A − [addr16 + Y] − $\bar{C}$	absolute indexed

```
S  V  D  I  Z  C
/  /  —  —  /  /
```

SEC   Set carry flag

	38	1	C ← 1	implied

```
S  V  D  I  Z  C
—  —  —  —  —  1
```

SED $ Set decimal mode

	F8	1		implied

```
S  V  D  I  Z  C
—  —  1  —  —  —
```

SE1   Set interrupt disable flag

	78	1		implied

```
S  V  D  I  Z  C
—  —  —  1  —  —
```

STA   Store accumulator in memory

addr	85	2	[addr] ← A	zero-page direct
addr16	8D	3	[addr16] ← A	absolute direct
addr,X	95	2	[addr + X] ← A	zero-page indexed
(addr,X)	81	2	[[addr + X]] ← A	pre-indexed indirect
(addr),Y	91	2	[[addr + 1, addr] + Y] ← A	post-indexed indirect
addr16,X	9D	3	[addr16 + X] ← A	absolute indexed
addr16,Y	99	3	[addr16 + Y] ← A	absolute indexed

```
S  V  D  I  Z  C
—  —  —  —  —  —
```

STX   Store X-register in memory

addr	86	2	[addr] ← X	zero-page direct
addr,Y	96	2	[addr + Y] ← X	zero-page indexed
addr16	8E	3	[addr16] ← X	absolute direct

```
S  V  D  I  Z  C
—  —  —  —  —  —
```

STY   Store Y-register in memory

addr	84	2	[addr] ← Y	zero-page direct
addr,X	94	2	[addr + X] ← Y	zero-page indexed
addr16	8C	3	[addr16] ← Y	absolute indirect

```
S  V  D  I  Z  C
—  —  —  —  —  —
```

TAX		Transfer accumulator to X-register	
	AA 1	X ← A	implied
		S V D I Z C	
		/ — — — / —	
TAY		Transfer accumulator to Y	
	A8 1	Y ← A	implied
		S V D I Z C	
		/ — — — / —	
TSX		Transfer SP to X-register	
	BA 1	SP ← X	implied
		S V D I Z C	
		/ — — — / —	
TXA		Transfer X-register to A	
	8A 1	A ← X	implied
		S V D I Z C	
		/ — — — / —	
TYA		Transfer Y-register to A	
	98 1	Y ← A	implied
		S V D I Z C	
		/ — — — / —	

Example Programs

1. 16 bit addition

This program adds 2 16-bit numbers, storing the result in 2 bytes.

Sample:

(0046) = 1C	We wish to add the two numbers stored in
(0047) = F0	locations 46-47 and 48-49 and place the result
(0048) = 2D	in locations 50-51.
(0049) = 0E	
(0050) = result	
(0051)	

F01C + 0E2D = FE49

Assembly language

```
CLC       — carry must be 0 for least significant bytes
LDA $46   —
ADC $48   — add the two least significant bytes
STA $50   — and store least significant byte of result
LDA $47
ADC $49   — add the two most significant bytes and carry
STA $51   — store resultant byte
BRK       — stop
```

124

Machine code

```
$18
$A5 $46
$65 $48
$85 $50
$A5 $47
$65 $49
$85 $51
$00
```

You can enter this program by POKEing the machine code values and performing a SYS command. Use PEEKs to check that the correct result was obtained.

2. Using a table and index register

This program uses a previously set up table to find the square of a number, which is then stored.

Sample:

$$(\$0050) = \$06 \quad — \text{ number to be squared}$$
$$(\$0051) = \$24 \quad — \text{ result}$$

table starts at $0060 — the first byte contains 0^2, the second 1^2, the third 2^2, etc.

Assembly language

```
LDX $50      — number to be squared is used as an index
               into the table
LDA $60,X    — put the square into the accumulator
STA $51      — store it
BRK
```

Machine code

```
$A6 $50
$B5 $60
$85 $51
$00
```

Tables can be useful in avoiding complex calculations during a program run. The disadvantage is that you must do the caulculations and store the results in memory (or have another program or program section do it for you). Also, tables take up memory which you may not be able to afford. Thus tables are a trade-off between memory usage and speed.

3. Loops

This program adds a series of numbers and stores the result. Note the use of a label to indicate the start of the loop in the assembly language version. This is converted to a branch displacement in machine code.

Sample:

($0050) = $04	— number of numbers to be added
($0051) = $16	— start of series
$0052) = $2E	
($0053) = $10	
($0054) = $2C	— end of series
($0055) = result	

Assembly language

	LDA # 0	— initialize sum to 0
	TAX	— initialize loop counter to 0
SUM	CLC	— start of loop; don't include carry
	ADC $51,X	— add next number to current sum
	INX	— increment counter by 1
	CPX $50	— is counter equal to length of series?
	BNE SUM	— no : go to start of loop
	STA $55	— yes : store result
	BRK	— stop.

Machine code

$A9 $00	
$AA	
$18	
$75 $51	
$E8	
$E4 $50	
$D0 $F8	— branch displacement −8
$85 $55	
$00	

Interrupt-driven subroutines

Sixty times a second a hardware interrupt occurs. It is possible to add your own machine code routines to the interrupt routines. In this way you can seemingly run two different tasks simultaneously, or use interrupt-driven subroutines to carry out parts of the main program.

The procedure is as follows:
1)   Load the machine code routine into memory
2)   Disable interrupts
3)   Load the address of your machine code routine into locations 788, 789 (in the usual low-byte, high-byte format)
4)   Enable interrupts

The machine code routine must end with a jump to the normal ROM interrupt handling routine at $EABF.

Once the interrupt vector has been set to point to your machine code, that routine is independent of BASIC. STOP and RESTORE will reset the vector to $EABF and deactivate your machine code.

The following example program uses an interrupt driven subroutine to move a character around the screen. The S and F keys control left, and right movements respectively.

```
10 PRINT "<CLR>"
20 POKE 52,28 : POKE 56,28 : CLR
30 FOR J=38400 TO  38905 : POKE J,2 :  NEXT :REM Set  Colour
Mem
40 POKE 7935,42
50 POKE 251,255 : POKE 252,30 : REM Init Char Posn
60 FOR J=7168 TO 7282 : READ C : POKE J,C : NEXT : REM Poke
   in Machine Code
70 SYS 7270
80 GOTO 80
90 REM Remove Char from Screen
95 DATA 169,32,160,0,145,251
100 REM Get Key
110 DATA 165,197,201,64,208,3,76,95,28,201,41,240,
        7,201,42,240,39,76,95,28
120 REM Move Left
130 DATA 169,0,197,251,208,17,169,30,197,252,208,11,
        169,249,133,251,169,31
140 DATA 133,252,76,95,28,198,251,169,255,197,251,
        208,2,198,252,76,95,28
150 REM Right Move
160 DATA 169,249,197,251,208,17,169,31,197,252,208,
        11,169,0,133,251,169,30,133,252
170 DATA 76,95,28,230,251,169,0,197,251,208,2,230,252
180 REM Put Char On Screen
190 DATA 169,42,145,251,76,191,234
200 REM Change Interrupt Vector
210 DATA 120,169,0,141,20,3,169,28,141,21,3,88,96
```

```
7168 169  32              LDA #32
7170 160   0              LDY #0
7172 145 251              STA (SA),Y    ; make char disappear
7174 165 197              LDA 197       ; get keystroke
7176 201  64              CMP #64       ; anything?
7178 208   3              BNE 3         ; yes
7180  76  95  28          JMP Appear    ; no
7183 201  41              CMP #41       ; "S"?
7185 240   7              BEQ Left      ; yes
7187 201  42              CMP #42       ; "F"?
7189 240  39              BEQ Right     ; yes
7191  76  95  28          JMP Appear    ; any other character
7194 169   0      Left =  LDA #0        ; check whether char
7196 197 251              CMP SA        ; is at top left
7198 208  17              BNE L1        ; of screen
7200 169  30              LDA #30       ;
7202 197 252              CMP SA+1      ;
7204 208  11              BNE LI        ; no
7206 169 249              LDA #249      ; yes - move char
7208 133 251              STA SA        ; to bottom right
7210 169  31              LDA #31       ; of screen
7212 133 252              STA SA+1      ;
7214  76  95  28          JMP Appear    ;
7217 198 251      LI =    DEC SA        ; ordinary move left
7219 169 255              LDA #255      ; check whether
7221 197 251              CMP SA        ; crossed page
                                        ; boundary
7223 208   2              BNE L2        ; no
7225 198 252              DEC SA+1      ; yes - change page
7227  76  95  28  L2 =    JMP Appear    ;
7230 169 249      Right = LDA #249      ; check whether char
7232 197 251              CMP SA        ; at bottom right of
                                        ; screen
7234 208  17              BNE L3        ; no
7236 169 31               LDA #31       ;
7238 197 252              CMP SA+1      ;
7240 208  11              BNE L3        ; no
7242 169   0              LDA #0        ; yes-move it to top
7244 133 251              STA SA        ; left of screen
7246 169 30               LDA #30       ;
7248 133 252              STA SA+1      ;
7250  76  95  28          JMP Appear    ;
7253 230 251      L3 =    INC SA        ; normal move right
7255 169   0              LDA #0        ; crossed page bound?
7257 197 251              CMP SA        ;
7259 208   2              BNE 2         ; no
7261 230 252              INC SA+1      ; yes-change page
7263 169  42      Appear = LDA #42      ;
7265 145 251              STA (SA),Y    ; make char appear
7267  76 191 234          JMP $EABF     ; jump to ROM
                                        ; interrupt routine
7270 120                  SEI           ; disable interrupts
7271 169   0              LDA #0        ; change interrupt
7273 141  20   3          STA 788       ; vector to 7168
7276 169  28              LDA #28       ;
7278 141  21   3          STA 789       ;
7281  88                  CLI           ; enable interrupts
7282  96                  RTS           ;
```

MACHINE CODE TO DATA PROGRAM

After you finish writing you machine code in assembler, this BASIC program will convert your machine code into a series of DATA statements which is easily SAVED and LOADED. The program asks for the location of the machine code in memory and then for its length. The program will then convert your machine code to DATA statements. If everything is to your satisfaction, then lines 10-99 should be deleted for proper operation of the loader.

```
10 INPUT"ENTER START OF  MACHINE CODE";A: INPUT"ENTER  LENGTH
OF CODE";L
15  PRINT" 🅲 🅒 🅒 🅒100S="MID$(STR$(A),2)":F ☐I=8TOS+"MID$(STR
$(L-1),2)":READX:C=C+X:";
20 PRINT"P ☐,X:NEXT":L=A+L:LI=120:T=A:GOTO90
30 PRINT" 🅲 🅒 🅒":FORT=ATOT+32STEP8:IFT=LTHEN96
40              PRINTLI"D ☑";:LI=LI+10:FORI=OTO7:X=PEEK(T+I):
IFT+I=LTHEN94
50 PRINTMID$(STR$(X),2)",";:C=C+X:NEXT:PRINT" ▓ ":NEXT
90 FORI=631TO638:POKEI,13:NEXT:POKE198,7
92 PRINT"LI="LI:A="T":L="L":C="C":6 ☐30 🅢":END
94 IFI<>8THENPRINT" ▓ ":I=S:NEXT
96 T=A+32:NEXT
97              PRINT"110IFC<>"MID$(STR$(C),2)"T ☐?"CHR$(34)"DATA
ERROR!!"CHR$(34)":E/
98 FORI=631638:POKEI,13:NEXT
99 POKE198,7:PRINT"L 🅢 🅢":END
```

PLOT PROGRAM

Plot program for an unexpanded VIC-20. This routine which is called from BASIC will move the cursor to any position on the screen you specify. If you wish to locate the routine at address other than 7600, then lines 95 to 100 should be changed. Line 95 simply lowers the top of memory pointers so that "PLOT" is not clobbered by BASIC. For VIC's with extra RAM, these pointers should be changed. If these pointers are changed, then the address where the routine is located should also be changed (in line 100). The version listed here is for an unexpanded VIC and changes for a VIC with 8K RAM are included at the end of the routine.

```
50 REM MACHINE CODE  FOR  PLOT   (TOTALLY RELOCATBLE) FOR THE
VIC 20
55 REM FOR THE UNEXPANDED VIC
60 REM FORMAT IS: SYSPLOT(X,Y)
70 REM WHERE PLOT=ADDRESS OF MACHINE CODE ROUTINE
80 REM        X=X COORDINATE OF CURSOR (ACROSS SCREEN)
90 REM        Y=Y COORDINATE OF CURSOR (DOWN SCREEN)
95 POKE55,177:POKE56,29
100 S=7600:FORI=STOS+26:READX:C=C+X:POKEI,X:NEXT
110 IFC<>3835THENPRINT"DATA ERROR!!":END
120 DATA32,250,206,32,158,215,138,72
130 DATA32,253,206,32,158,215,138,72
140 DATA32,247,206,104,170,104,168,24
150 DATA76,240,255
```

For a VIC with 8K RAM, change lines 55, 95, and 100 to:

```
55 REM FOR VIC-20 WITH 8K RAM
95 POKE55,228:POKE56,63
100 S=16357:FORI=STOS+26:READX:C=C+X:POKEI,X:NEXT
```

For memory configurations other than the unexpanded and 8K VIC, the pointers should be changed accordingly. To use the routine, first type in the program and then save it as "PLOT". PLOT may be used in direct or program mode. In both cases, the loader which pokes the data into memory must be executed. To use the routine, in either direct mode or program mode, type SYS PLOT (x,y), where x=no. of characters across screen and y=no. of characters down the screen. For the unexpanded VIC, PLOT=7600 and for an 8K VIC, PLOT=16357.

e.g.   SYS7600 (5, 10) : PRINT "HI THERE!"

The above example (for an unexpanded VIC) will move the cursor 5 locations to the right and 10 locations down from the top left hand corner of the screen. For an 8K VIC, change 7600 to 16357.

Appendix A

1) CHR$ Value Codes

Character	CHR$ Code	Character	CHR$ Code
	0	#	35
	1	$	36
	2	%	37
STOP	3	&	38
	4	,	39
WHITE	5	(	40
	6	)	41
	7	*	42
	8	+	43
	9	,	44
	10	–	45
	11	.	46
	12	/	47
RETURN	13	0	48
Lower case switch	14	1	49
	15	2	50
	16	3	51
CRSR ↓	17	4	52
RVS ON	18	5	53
CLR/HOME	19	6	54
INST/DEL	20	7	55
	21	8	56
	22	9	57
	23	÷	58
	24	;	59
	25	<	60
	26	=	61
	27	>	62
RED	28	?	63
CRSR →	29	@	64
GREEN	30	A	65
BLUE	31	B	66
space	32	C	67
!	33	D	68
"	34	E	69

Character	CHR$ Code	Character	CHR$ Code
F	70	◳	109
G	71	◲	110
H	72	▫	111
I	73	▫	112
J	74	◼	113
K	75	▤	114
L	76	♥	115
M	77	▥	116
N	78	◰	117
O	79	⊠	118
P	80	◧	119
Q	81	✚	120
R	82	▯	121
S	83	◆	122
T	84	⊞	123
U	85	▣	124
V	86	▥	125
W	87	π	126
X	88	◣	127
Y	89		128
Z	90		129
[	91		130
£	92	SHIFT RUN/STOP	131
]	93		132
↑	94	f1	133
←	95	f3	134
▦	96	f5	135
♠	97	f7	136
▥	98	f2	137
▤	99	f4	138
▤	100	f6	139
▭	101	f8	140
▥	102	SHIFT RETURN	141
▥	103	Upper case switch	142
▥	104		143
◱	105	BLACK	144
◰	106	CRSR ↑	145
◲	107	RVS OFF	146
▫	108	CLR/HOME	147

Character	CHR$ Code	Character	CHR$ Code
INST/DEL	148	▢	170
	149	▢	171
	150	▢	172
	151	▢	173
	152	▢	174
	153	▢	175
	154	▢	176
	155	▢	177
PURPLE	156	▢	178
CRSR ←	157	▢	179
YELLOW	158	▢	180
CYAN	159	▢	181
space	160	▢	182
▢	161	▢	183
▢	162	▢	184
▢	163	▢	185
▢	164	▢	186
▢	165	▢	187
▢	166	▢	188
▢	167	▢	189
▢	168	▢	190
▢	169	▢	191

Codes 192-223 are the same as 96-127
Codes 224-254 are the same as 160-190
Code 255 is the same as code 126

---

2) Screen Codes

Character Set 1	Character Set 2	Screen Code
@		0
A	a	1
B	b	2
C	c	3
D	d	4
E	e	5
F	f	6
G	g	7

Character Set 1	Character Set 2	Screen Code
H	h	8
I	i	9
J	j	10
K	k	11
L	l	12
M	m	13
N	n	14
O	o	15
P	p	16
Q	q	17
R	r	18
S	s	19
T	t	20
U	u	21
V	v	22
W	w	23
X	x	24
Y	y	25
Z	z	26
[		27
£		28
]		29
↑		30
←		31
space		32
!		33
"		34
#		35
$		36
%		37
&		38
'		39
(		40
)		41
*		42
+		43
,		44
-		45
.		46
/		47

Character Set 1	Character Set 2	Screen Code
0		48
1		49
2		50
3		51
4		52
5		53
6		54
7		55
8		56
9		57
:		58
;		59
<		60
=		61
>		62
?		63
		64
♠	A	65
	B	66
	C	67
	D	68
	E	69
	F	70
	G	71
	H	72
	I	73
	J	74
	K	75
	L	76
	M	77
	N	78
	O	79
	P	80
	Q	81
	R	82
♥	S	83
	T	84
	U	85
⊠	V	86

Character Set 1	Character Set 2	Screen Code
▣	W	87
♣	X	88
▢	Y	89
◆	Z	90
⊞		91
▨		92
▯		93
π	▓	94
◣	▨	95
space		96
▮		97
▬		98
▃		99
▯		100
▢		101
▓		102
▯		103
▩		104
◢	▨	105
▯		106
⊞		107
◩		108
◪		109
◪		110
▭		111
◪		112
⊟		113
⊞		114
◪		115
▯		116
▮		117
▪		118
▢		119
▢		120
▬		121
▢		122
◪		123
◩		124
◪		125

136

Character Set 1	Character Set 2	Screen Code
◪		126
◪		127

Codes 128-255 produce reversed images of codes 0-127

---

3) ASCII Codes

Character	Code	Character	Code
NULL	0	GS	29
SOH	1	RS	30
STX	2	US	31
ETX	3	space	32
EOT	4	!	33
ENQ	5	"	34
ACK	6	#	35
BEL	7	$	36
BS	8	%	37
HT	9	&	38
LF	10	'	39
VT	11	(	40
FF	12	)	41
CR	13	*	42
SO	14	+	43
SI	15	,	44
DLE	16	-	45
DC1	17	.	46
DC2	18	/	47
DC3	19	0	48
DC4	20	1	49
NAK	21	2	50
SYN	22	3	51
ETB	23	4	52
CAN	24	5	53
EM	25	6	54
SUB	26	7	55
ESC	27	8	56
FS	28	9	57

Character	Code	Character	Code
≑	58	a	97
;	59	b	98
<	60	c	99
=	61	d	100
>	62	e	101
?	63	f	102
@	64	g	103
A	65	h	104
B	66	i	105
C	67	j	106
D	68	k	107
E	69	l	108
F	70	m	109
G	71	n	110
H	72	o	111
I	73	p	112
J	74	q	113
K	75	r	114
L	76	s	115
M	77	t	116
N	78	u	117
O	79	v	118
P	80	w	119
Q	81	x	120
R	82	y	121
S	83	z	122
T	84	;	123
U	85	<	124
V	86	=	125
W	87	>	126
X	88	DEL	127
Y	89		
Z	90		
[	91		
\	92		
]	93		
↑	94		
←	95		
space	96		

Appendix B

Memory
Complete Map

Address (Decimal)	Description
0	Jump for USR
1 - 2	Vector for USR
3 - 4	Floating point - fixed point vector
5 - 6	Fixed point - floating point vector
7	BASIC counter. Search character ':' or end of line
8	Scan-quotes flag
9	Column position of cursor on line
10	Flag ; 0 = LOAD, 1 = VERIFY
11	BASIC input buffer pointer ; subscript number
12	Default DIM flag
13	Variable type flag : FF = string, 00 = numeric
14	Numeric type flag : 80 = integer, 00 = floating point
15	DATA scan flag : LIST quote flag ; memory flag
16	Subscript flag ; FNx flag
17	Flag ; 0 = INPUT, 152 = READ, 64 = GET
18	ATN sign flag ; comparison evaluation flag
19	Current I/O prompt flag
20 - 21	Where BASIC stores integers used in calculations
22	Temporary string stack pointer
23 - 24	Last temporary string vector
25 - 33	Stack for temporary string descriptors
34 - 37	Utility pointer area
43 - 44	Pointer to start of BASIC program
45 - 46	Pointer to end of BASIC program ; start of BASIC variables
47 - 48	Pointer to end of variables ; start of arrays
51 - 52	Pointer to start of string storage - strings move down from top of available memory towards arrays.
53 - 54	Pointer to end of string storage
55 - 56	Pointer to top of RAM available to BASIC
57 - 58	Current BASIC line number
59 - 60	Previous BASIC line number
61 - 62	Pointer to BASIC statement (for CONT)
63 - 64	Current DATA line number
65 - 66	Pointer to current DATA item
67 - 68	Jump vector for INPUT statement
69 - 70	Current variable name

71 - 72	Current variable address
73 - 74	Variable pointer for FOR/NEXT statement
75 - 76	Y save ; operator save ; BASIC pointer save
77	Comparison symbol
78 - 79	Work area ; function definition pointer
80 - 81	Work area ; string descriptor pointer
82	Length of string
83	Garbage collect use
84 - 86	Jump vector for functions
87 - 96	Numeric work area
97 - 102	Floating point accumulator 1 ; Exponent, 4 byte Mantissa, Sign
103	Series evaluation constant pointer
104	Accumulator 1 overflow
105 - 110	Floating point accumulator 2
111	Sign comparison - Acc 1 with Acc 2
112	Acc 2 rounding
113 - 114	Cassette buffer length ; series pointer
115 - 138	CHRGOT BASIC subroutine - gets next BASIC character
139 - 143	RND storage and work area
144	ST - status byte
145	STOP and REVERSE flags ; Keyswitch PIA
146	Timing constant for tape
147	Flag : 0 = LOAD, 1 = VERIFY
148	Serial output ; deferred character flag
150	Tape EOT received
151	Register save
152	Number of OPEN files
153	Current input device
154	Current output (CMD) device
155	Tape character parity
156	Flag : byte received
157	Output control flag : direct = 128 ; run = 0
158	Tape pass 1 error log
159	Tape pass 2 error log
160 - 162	Jiffie clock - TI and TI$ use this
163	Serial bit count
164	Cycle count
165	Tape write bit count
166	Pointer to tape buffer
167	Tape write count ; input bit storage
168	Tape write new byte ; Read error ; input bit count
169	Write start bit ; Read bit error
170	Tape scan ; count
171	Write read length ; Read checksum ; parity

140

172 - 173	Pointer to tape buffer ; scrolling
174 - 175	Tape end addresses ; end of program
176 - 177	Tape timing constants
178 - 179	Pointer to start of tape buffer
180	Tape timer ; bit count
181	Tape EOR ; RS-232 next bit out
182	Read character error ; next byte out
183	Number of characters in current file name
184	Current logical file number
185	Current secondary address
186	Current device number
187 - 188	Pointer to current file name
189	Write shift byte ; Read input character
190	Number of blocks remaining to Read/Write
191	Serial word buffer
192	Tape motor interlock
193 - 194	I/O start addresses
195 - 196	KERNAL setup pointer
197	Current key pressed (see Appendix H)
198	Keyboard buffer counter
199	Flag : screen reverse - 1 is on, 0 is off
200	Pointer to end-of-line for input
201 - 202	Cursor log (row, column)
203	Current key pressed
204	Flag : cursor blink enable (0 is on)
205	Cursor blink delay
206	Character under cursor
207	Flag : cursor on/off
208	Input from screen/keyboard
209 - 210	Pointer to screen line on which cursor appears
211	Position of cursor on line
212	0 = direct cursor, else programmed
213	Screen line length, 21, 43, 65, 87
214	Current screen line number - To change cursor position, 201, 210, 211 and 214 must be changed
215	ASCII value of last keypress
216	Number of INSERTs outstanding
217 - 240	Screen line link table
241	Dummy screen line link
242	Screen row marker
243 - 244	Pointer to current location in colour memory
245 - 246	Pointer to keyscan table
247 - 248	Pointer to RS-232 receiver buffer start
249 - 250	Pointer to RS-232 transmitter buffer start
251 - 254	Free zero-page locations
255	BASIC storage

256 - 266	Float - ASCII work area
256 - 318	Tape error log
256 - 511	Processor stack area
512 - 600	BASIC input buffer
601 - 610	Logical file table for OPEN files
611 - 620	Device number table for OPEN files
621 - 630	Secondary address table
631 - 640	Keyboard buffer
641 - 642	Pointer to start of memory for operating system
643 - 644	Pointer to end of memory for operating system
645	Serial bus timeout flag
646	Current colour code (for PRINTed character)
647	Colour under cursor
648	Screen memory page indicator
649	Maximum length of keyboard buffer - must be less than 11
650	Key autorepeat (0 = cursor controls, 255 = all)
651	Pre-repeat delay
652	Inter-repeat delay
653	Keyboard flag for SHIFT, CTRL and ◖ keys. If SHIFT pressed, bit 0 is set, if CTRL, bit 1, if ◖, bit 2
654	Last shift pattern
655 - 656	Pointer for keyboard table set-up
657	Shift mode (0 = enabled, 128 = disabled)
658	Auto scroll down flag (0 = on, else off)
659	RS-232 control register
660	RS-232 command register
661 - 662	Non-standard (bit time/2 − 100)
663	RS-232 status register
664	Number of bits to send
665 - 666	Baud rate (full) bit time
667	Pointer to RS-232 receiver buffer (end)
668	Pointer to RS-232 receiver buffer (start)
669	Pointer to RS-232 transmit buffer (start)
670	Pointer to RS-232 transmit buffer (end)
671 - 672	Holds IRQ during tape operations
673 - 767	Program indirects
768 - 769	Error message link
770 - 771	Basic warm start link
772 - 773	Tokenization routine link
774 - 775	Print tokens link
776 - 777	Start new BASIC code link
778 - 779	Get arithmetic element link
780	Temporary storage of A during SYS
781	Temporary storage of X during SYS

782	Temporary storage of Y during SYS
783	Temporary storage of P during SYS
788 - 789	Hardware interrupt vector (EABF)
790 - 791	Break (BRK) interrupt vector (FED2)
792 - 793	NMI interrupt vector (FEAD)
794 - 795	OPEN vector (F40A)
796 - 797	CLOSE vector (F34A)
798 - 799	Set input device vector (F2C7)
800 - 801	Set output device vector (F309)
802 - 803	Restore I/O vector (F3F3)
804 - 805	Input vector (F20E)
806 - 807	Output vector (F27A)
808 - 809	Test STOP-key vector (F770)
810 - 811	GET vector (F1F5)
812 - 813	Close all files vector (F3EF)
814 - 815	User vector (FED2)
816 - 817	Load-from-device vector (F549)
818 - 819	Save to device vector (F549)
828 - 1019	Cassette buffer - useful for holding machine code when no files are being used
1024 - 4095	3K expansion area
4096 - 7679	User BASIC area
7680 - 8191	Screen memory
8192 - 16383	Expansion 1 (8K)
16384 - 24575	Expansion 2 (8K)
24576 - 32767	Expansion 3 (8K)
32768 - 36863	Character generator ROM
36864 - 37887	I/O Block 0
36864 - 36879	Address of VIC chip registers
36864	bits 0 - 6 - horizontal centering ; bit 7 - interface scan
36865	vertical centering
36866	bits 0 - 6 - number of columns ; bit 7 - part of video matrix address
36867	bits 1 - 6 - number of rows ; bit 0 - 8x8 or 16x8 characters
36868	TV raster beam line
36869	bits 0 - 3 - start of character memory ; bits 4 - 7 - rest of video address
36870	light pen position - horizontal
36871	light pen position - vertical
36872	Paddle X value
36873	Paddle Y value
36874	Tone register (low)
36875	Tone register (mid)
36876	Tone register (high)

36877	Noise register
36878	bits 0-3 - volume ; bits 4-7 - auxialiary colour
36879	bits 4-7 - background colour ; bits 0-2 - border colour ; bit 3 - inverted/normal mode (see Appendix E)
37136 - 37151	6522 VIA 1
37136	Port B output register (user port and RS-232 lines)
37137	Port A output register
37138	Data direction register B
37139	Data direction register A
37140	Timer 1 low byte
37141	Timer 1 high byte and counter
37142	Timer 1 low byte
37143	Timer 1 high byte
37144	Timer 2 low byte
37145	Timer 2 high byte
37146	Shift register
37147	Auxiliary control register
37148	Peripheral control register
37149	Interrupt flag register
37150	Interrupt enable register
37151	Port A (sense cassette switch)
37152 - 37167	6522 VIA 2
37152	Port B output register
37153	Port A output register
37154	DDR B
37155	DDR A
37156	Timer 1, low byte latch
37157	Timer 1, high byte latch
37158	Timer 1, low byte counter
37159	Timer 1, high byte counter (Timer 1 used for 60/sec interrupt)
37160	Timer 2, low byte latch
37161	Timer 2, high byte latch
37162	Shift register
37163	Auxiliary control register
37164	Peripheral control register
37165	Interrupt flag register
37166	Interrupt enable register
37167	Port A output register
37888 - 38399	Location of colour memory with 8K + expansion
38400 - 38911	Colour memory (unexpanded or 3K expansion)
38912 - 39935	I/O block 2
39936 - 40959	I/O block 3
40960 - 49152	Expansion

```
49152 - 57343    BASIC ROM
57344 - 65535    KERNAL ROM
```

Appendix C

Keyboard Graphics and how to get them.

Symbol	Keypress	Symbol	Keypress
▨	C= E **	▦	C= R
◱	C= W	◨	C= Q
◲	C= D	◳	C= F
◰	C= C	◰	C= V
◪	C= B	▨	C= +
▢	C= T	▢	C= Y
▬	C= U	▬	C= I
▭	C= O	▭	C= P
▯	C= @	◧	C= –
▫	C= G	▫	C= H
◫	C= J	▮	C= K
◫	C= L	◡	C= N
◫	C= M	▱	C= £
◲	C= S	▥	C= X
◰	C= A	◩	C= Z
◣	C= *		
▢	SHIFT L	▢	SHIFT @
▢	SHIFT O	▢	SHIFT P
◲	SHIFT I	◰	SHIFT U
◪	SHIFT K	◩	SHIFT J
◘	SHIFT W	▩	SHIFT Q
⊞	SHIFT +	⊠	SHIFT V
◩	SHIFT M	◿	SHIFT N
◆	SHIFT Z	♥	SHIFT S
♣	SHIFT X	♠	SHIFT A
▢	SHIFT E	▢	SHIFT D
▤	SHIFT *	▤	SHIFT C
▤	SHIFT F	▢	SHIFT R
▯	SHIFT T	▯	SHIFT G
▯	SHIFT B	▯	SHIFT –
▯	SHIFT H	▯	SHIFT Y
◪	SHIFT ●		
↑	UP ARROW	←	LEFT ARROW
π	PI		

As well as these there are a set of symbols used to represent control characters such as color controls and cursor controls.

The symbols vary depending upon whether the computer is in upper case or lower case mode.

The symbols are:

Upper case.

Symbol	Keypress
▨	CLR
▨	HOME
▨	cursor down
▢	cursor up
▨	cursor right
▮▮	cursor left
▬	ctrl 1
▨	ctrl 2
▨	ctrl 3
◣	ctrl 4
▨	ctrl 5
▨	ctrl 6
◧	ctrl 7
▨	ctrl 8
▨	ctrl 9
▬	ctrl 0

Lower case

Symbol	Keypress
▨	HOME
▨	cursor down
▨	ctrl 2
▨	ctrl 4
▨	ctrl 8
▨	ctrl 9

**   The ⟨C symbol is the special shift key
located to the left of the left hand shift
key

147

Appendix D

Useful ROM routines

The KERNAL is the operating system of the VIC 20. It contains many subroutines which can be of use to the machine language programmer. All of these can be accessed using a JSR instruction. Control will be returned to your program after the KERNAL subroutine has executed. In the brief descriptions of these subroutines below, the following information is presented.

Name, Purpose
Address : in hex
Communication registers : registers used to pass information to and from the KERNAL subroutine.
Preparatory routines : these routines must be called prior to the subroutine in question.
Possible errors : if an error occurs, when the subroutine returns the carry flag will be set, and the error code will be in the accumulator.
Stack : number of bytes of stack used by the routine.
Registers used : a list of all registers used by the KERNAL routine.

1) Name : ACPTR
   Purpose : Get data from serial bus
   Address : $FFA5
   Communication registers : A; data returned in accumulator
   Prep. routines : TALK, TKSA
   Possible errors : see READST
   Stack : 13
   Registers used : X, A

2) Name : CHKIN
   Purpose : Open a channel for input
   Address : $FFC6
   Communication registers : X; load X with number of logical file to be used
   Prep routines : OPEN
   Possible errors : 3,5,6
   Stack : 0
   Registers used : A,X

3) Name : CHKOUT
   Purpose : Open a channel for output
   Address : $FFC9
   Communication registers : X; load X with logical file number to be used
   Prep. routines : OPEN
   Possible errors : 3,5,7
   Stack : 0
   Registers used : A,X

4) Name : CHRIN
   Purpose : Get a character from input channel
   Address : $FFCF
   Communication registers : A; data byte returned in A
   Prep. routines : OPEN, CHKIN (unless device is keyboard)
   Possible errors : see READST
   Stack : 0
   Registers used : A,X

5) Name : CHROUT
   Purpose : Output a character
   Address : $FFD2
   Communication registers : A; load byte to be output in A
   Prep. routines : OPEN,CHKOUT (unless device is screen)
   Possible errors : see READST
   Stack : 0
   Registers used : A

6) Name : CIOUT
   Purpose : Transmit a byte over the serial bus
   Address : $FFA8
   Communication registers : A; load byte to be output in A
   Prep. routines : LISTEN, (SECOND if device needs secondary
                    address)
   Possible errors : see READST
   Stack : 0
   Registers used : A

7) Name : CLALL
   Purpose : Close all files
   Address : $FFE7
   Communciation registers : none
   Prep. routines : none
   Possible errors : none
   Stack : 11
   Registers used : A,X

8) Name : CLOSE
   Purpose : Close a logical file
   Address $FFC3
   Communication registers : A; load A with logical file number to be
                    closed
   Prep. routines : none
   Possible errors : none
   Stack : 0
   Registers used : A,X

9) Name : CLRCHIN
   Purpose : Clear I/O channels
   Address : $FFCC
   Communication registers : none
   Prep. routines : none

Possible errors : none
Stack : 9
Registers used : A, X

10) Name : GETIN
Purpose : Get a character from keyboard buffer
Address : $FFE4
Communication registers : A; character code returned in A
Prep. routines : none
Possible errors : none
Stack : 0
Registers used : A, X

11) Name : IOBASE
Purpose : Define I/O memory page
Address : $FFF3
Communication registers : X, Y; respectively low and high addres
bytes of memory section where memor
mapped I/O devices are located ar
returned in X, Y
Prep. routines : none
Possible errors : none
Stack : Two registers used : X, Y

12) Name : LISTEN
Purpose : Command a device on the serial bus to receive data
Address : $FFB1
Communication registers : A; load A with number 4 - 31 indicating
device.
Prep. routines : none
Possible errors : see READST
Stack : 0
Registers used : A

13) Name : LOAD
Purpose : Load RAM from device, or verify
Address : $FFD5
Communication registers : A; set to 0 for load, 1 for verify. X, Y; low
and high bytes of starting address of load
Prep. routines : SETLFS, SETNAM
Possible errors : 0,4,5,8,9
Stack : 0
Registers used : A,X,Y

14) Name : MEMBOT
Purpose : Set or read the address of the bottom of RAM
Address : $FF9C
Communication registers : Carry flag; 1 to read, 0 to set bottom of
memory. X, Y; low and high bytes of
address. If carry is set, the address will
be returned in X, Y. If carry clear,

address in X, Y will be transferred to pointer to bottom of RAM

Prep. routines : none
Possible errors : none
Stack : 0
Registers used : X, Y, P

15) Name: MEMTOP
Purpose : Set or read the address of top of RAM
Address : $FF99
Communication registers : Carry, X, Y; as for MEMBOT
Prep. routines : none
Possible errors : none
Stack : 2
Registers used : X, Y, Carry

16) Name : OPEN
Purpose : Open a logical file
Address : $FFC0
Communication registers : none
Prep. routines : SETLFS, SETNAM
Possible errors : 1,2,4,5,6
Stack : 0
Registers used : A, X, Y

17) Name : PLOT
Purpose : Set cursor location or read cursor location
Address : $FFF0
Communication registers : Carry : 1 for set cursor location
0 for read cursor location
X; column number (0-21) returned to or loaded from
Y; row number (0-22) returned to or loaded from

Prep. routines : none
Possible errors : none
Stack : 2
Registers used : Carry, X, Y

18) Name : RDTIM
Purpose : Read system clock - 3 byte value
Address : $FFDE
Communication registers : A; most significant byte returned
X; next mostsignificant byte returned
Y; least significant byte returned

Prep. routines : none
Possible errors : none
Stack : 2
Registers used : A, X, Y

19) Name : READST
    Purpose : read status word
    Address $FFB7
    Communication registers : A; error code returned in A. See
    discussion of ST in BASIC section for
    codes and meanings
    Prep. routines : none
    Possible errors : none
    Stack : 2
    Registers used : A

20) Name : RESTOR
    Purpose : Restore default system and interrupt vectors
    Address : $FF8A
    Communication registers : none
    Prep. routines : none
    Possible errors : none
    Stack : 2
    Registers used : A, X, Y

21) Name : SAVE
    Purpose : Save memory to a device
    Address : $FFD8
    Communication registers : A; load with zero-page address. This
    address and the next byte contain the
    address of the start of memory to be
    saved.
    X, Y; low and high bytes of end address
    of memory to be saved.
    Prep. routines : SETLFS, SETNAM (SETNAM not needed if a
    nameless save to Datasette is desired)
    Possible errors : 5,8,9
    Stack : 0
    Registers used : A, X, Y

22) Name : SCNKEY
    Purpose : Scan the keyboard, put value in keyboard queue
    Address : $FF9F
    Communication registers : none
    Prep. routines : none
    Possible errors : none
    Stack : 0
    Registers used : A, X, Y

23) Name : SCREEN
    Purpose : Return number of screen rows and columns
    Address : $FFED
    Communication registers : X; number of columns returned in X
    Y; number of rows returned in Y
    Prep. routines : none
    Possible errors : none

Stack : 2
Registers used : X, Y

24) Name : SECOND
Purpose : Send secondary address for LISTEN
Address : $FF93
Communication registers : A; load with secondary address to be
sent
Prep. routines : LISTEN
Possible errors : see READST
Stack : 0
Registers used : A

25) Name : SETLFS
Purpose : Set up a logical file number, device and secondary
addresses
Address : $FFBA
Communication registers : A; load logical file number into A
X; device number
Y; command (secondary address)
Prep. routines : none
Possible errors : none
Stack : 2
Registers used : A, X, Y

26) Name : SETNAM
Purpose : Set up file name
Address : $FFBD
Communication registers : A; load length of file name into A
X, Y; low, high bytes of address of start of
memory where file name is stored
Prep. routines : none
Possible errors : none
Stack : 0
Registers used : A, X, Y

27) Name : SETTIM
Purpose : Set the system clock - 3 byte value
Address : $FFDB
Communication registers : A; most significant byte
X; next most significant byte
Y; least significant byte
Prep. routines : none
Possible errors : none
Stack : 2
Registers used : A, X, Y

28) Name : STOP
Purpose : Check if stop key pressed
Address : $FFE1

Communication registers : zero flag; set if STOP key pressed
Prep. routines : none
Possible errors : none
Stack : 0
Registers used : zero flag, A, X

29) Name : TALK
Purpose : Command a device on the serial bus to TALK
Address : $FFBA
Communication registers : A; load device number into A
Prep. routines : none
Possible errors : see READST
Stack : 0
Registers used : A

30) Name : TKSA
Purpose : send a secondary address to a device commanded to
TALK
Address : $FF96
Communication registers : A; load secondary address into A
Prep. routines : TALK
Possible errors : see READST
Stack : 0
Registers used : A

31) Name : UNLSN
Purpose : Command all devices on the serial bus to stop receiving
data
Address : $FFAE
Communication registers : none
Prep. routines : none
Possible errors : see READST
Stack : 0
Registers used : A

32) Name : UNTLK
Pupose : Send an UNTALK command to all devices on serial bus
Address : $FFAB
Communication registers : none
Prep. routines : none
Possible errors : see READST
Stack : 0
Registers used : A

33) Name : VECTOR
Purpose : Set or read system RAM vectors
Address : $FF8D
Communication registers : X, Y; address of list of system RAM
vectors
Carry flag; if set, the RAM vectors are

read into the list pointed to by X, Y and if clear, the contents of the list pointed to by X, Y are read into the RAM vectors.

Prep. routines : none
Possible errors : none
Stack : 2
Registers used : Carry flag, X, Y

Error Codes

Value	Meaning
0	Routine terminated by STOP key
1	Too many open files
2	File already open
3	File not open
4	File not found
5	Device not present
6	File is not an input file
7	File is not an output file
8	File name is missing
9	Illegal device number

Appendix E

Background/Border colour codes.

Location 36879 contains the code for colour combinations of the screen background and border.

Screen	Black	White	Red	Border Cyan	Purple	Green	Blue	Yellow
Black	8	9	10	11	12	13	14	15
White	24	25	26	27	28	29	30	31
Red	40	41	42	43	44	45	46	47
Cyan	56	57	58	59	60	61	62	63
Purple	72	73	74	75	76	77	78	79
Green	88	89	90	91	92	93	94	95
Blue	104	105	106	107	108	109	110	111
Yellow	120	121	122	123	124	125	126	127
Orange	136	137	138	139	140	141	142	143
Lt. Orange	152	153	154	155	156	157	158	159
Pink	168	169	170	171	172	173	174	175
Lt. Cyan	184	185	186	187	188	189	190	191
Lt. Purple	200	201	202	203	204	205	206	207
Lt. Green	216	217	218	219	220	221	222	223
Lt. Blue	232	233	234	235	236	237	238	239
Lt. Yellow	248	249	250	251	252	253	254	255

The default value is 27.

Appendix F

Memory Allocation

Address (decimal)		Address (hex)
0	BASIC working memory	0
1023	storage	3FF
0124	3K Memory	400
4095	Expansion	FFF
4096	User memory area (unexpanded or 3K exp)	1000
7679	Screen memory when 8K or greater expansion	1DFF
7680	Screen memory (unexpanded or 3K exp)	1E00
8185	User memory (8K or greater expansion)	1FF9
8192	8K Memory	2000
16383	Expansion	3FFF
16384	8K Memory	4000
24575	Expansion	5FFF
24576	8K Memory	6000
32767	Expansion	7FFF
32768	VIC20 Character Sets	8000
36836	(ROM)	8FFF
36864	6560 VIC Chip	9000
36879	Control registers	900F
37136	6522 VIA Chip	9110
37167	I/O Control registers	912F
37888	Colour Memory	9400
38399	(if memory is expanded)	95FF
38400	Colour Memory	9600
38911	(unexpanded system)	97FF
40960	Expansion ROM	A000
49151		BFFF
49152	BASIC interpreter	CP00
57343	(ROM)	DFFF
57344	KERNAL Operating System	E000
65535	(ROM)	FFFF

Appendix G

BASIC error messages

BASIC's error messages aren't always illuminating. This list of messages and explanations may be helpful.

BAD DATA:

The program expected numeric data, but received string data (from an OPENed file)

BAD SUBSCRIPT:

The program tried to reference an element of an array whose subscript was outside the dimensions of the array.

CAN'T CONTINUE:

CONT doesn't work because (a) the program was never run, (b) it stopped due to an error condition or (c) an attempt was made to edit the program.

DEVICE NOT PRESENT:

The relevant I/O device isn't present.

DIVISION BY ZERO:

Not allowed.

EXTRA IGNORED:

Too many data items typed in response to an INPUT statement. Only the required numer of items were accepted. Doesn't stop a program.

FILE ALREADY EXISTS:

The name of the source file being copied with the COPY statement alread exists on the destination diskette.

FILE NOT FOUND:

On tape, this means that an END-OF-TAPE marker was found, so search stops. On disk no such file exists.

FILE NOT OPEN:

You tried an I/O command on a file that hasn't been opened.

FILE OPEN:

You tried to open a file using a number assigned to a file already OPEN.

FORMULA TOO COMPLEX:

Either a string expression is too intricate, or an arithmetic expression is too complex. If it's a string, break it up into two parts. If it's an arithmetic expression, try using parentheses.

ILLEGAL DIRECT:

The command attempted in direct mode can only be used in program mode

ILLEGAL QUANTITY:

A number used as an argument is out of range. e.g. POKEing a value greater than 255.

LOAD:

Too many errors (> 31) were found on a tape LOAD

NEXT WITHOUT FOR:
Either you've put in too many NEXT statements, forgotten a FOR statement or branched past a FOR statement.

NOT INPUT FILE:
An attempt has been made to read from a file designated as output only.

NOT OUTPUT FILE:
An attempt has been made to write to a file designated as input only.

OUT OF DATA:
A READ statement has run out of data.

OUT OF MEMORY:
No more RAM left for program or variables. Also caused by too many nested FOR loops and/or GOSUBs. In this case you may have lots of memory but no stack left. You may also have inadvertently changed the top-of-memory pointer.

OVERFLOW:
The result of a calculation is greater than $1.70141884E+38$.

REDIM'D ARRAY:
An array name appears in more than one DIM statement, or has been both implicitly and explicitly DIMensioned.

REDO FROM START:
An INPUT statement received the wrong type of data. Doesn't stop the program, just continues prompting until the correct type of data is input.

RETURN WITHOUT GOSUB:
A RETURN for which there is no corresponding GOSUB. Usually caused by dropping into the subroutine inadvertently.

STRING TOO LONG:
Strings can be a maximum of 255 characters long.

SYNTAX:
BASIC doesn't recognise the statement.

TYPE MISMATCH:
Number used in place of string, or vice-versa.

UNDEF'D FUNCTION:
A user defined function was called but has not yet been defined, with a DEF FN statement

UNDEF'D STATEMENT:
An attempt has been made to go to a non-existent line number.

VERIFY:
The program on tape or disk being VERIFYd does not match the program in memory.

Appendix H

Current Key Depressed

Location 197 stores a coded value of the current key depressed. If more than one key is depressed the higher value is stored.

Key	Value	Key	Value	Key	Value	Key	Value
1	0	none	16	SPACE	32	Q	48
3	1	A	17	Z	33	E	49
5	2	D	18	C	34	T	50
7	3	G	19	B	35	U	51
9	4	J	20	M	36	O	52
+	5	L	21	•	37	@	53
£	6	;	22	none	38	↑	54
DEL	7	CRSR ←→	23	f1	39	f5	55
←	8	STOP	24	none	40	2	56
W	9	none	25	S	41	4	57
R	10	X	26	F	42	6	58
Y	11	V	27	H	43	8	59
I	12	N	28	K	44	0	60
P	13	,	29	:	45	—	61
*	14	/	30	=	46	HOME	62
RETURN	15	CRSR ↕	31	f3	47	f7	63

Appendix I

User callable BASIC routines available from Machine Language.

The machine language programmer can use the BASIC interpreter subroutines. This facility is invaluable since it saves the programmer time and memory. The following is a brief summary of some of the more useful routines.

NOTE: The VIC20 does all its calculations in floating point, using the two floating point accumulators (see memory map).

1. CIFL

- converts integer to floating point.
- To use:
    load Y-register with low byte of integer
    load A with high byte
    JSR $D391

Result returned in Floating Point Accumulator 1 (FPA 1).

- Note:
    The two byte integer is treated as signed;
    i.e. if bit 7 of the high byte is 1 the number is negative and in 2's complement; if 0 then positive.

2. CFLI

- converts floating point to integer.
- To use:
    call MVFPA1 (see below)
    JSR $D1BF

Result returned in $14, 15 (lo-byte, hi-byte) - in 2's complement if negative.

3. CANI

- converts ASCII number string to integer.
- To use:
    Put low byte of start address of string in $7A
    JSR $0079 (CHRGOT - scans string)
    JSR $C96B (CANI)

Result returned in $14, 15 (lo-byte, hi-byte) - in 2's complement if negative.

- Note:
    the ASCII number string must have a value less than 64000 and should be followed by a blank.

4. CANFL

- converts ASCII number string to floating point.
- To use:
    Put low byte of start address of string in $22
    Put high byte of start address of string in $23
    Load length of string in A

JSR $D6B5
Result returned in FPA1

5. CFLAN

- converts floating point to ASCII number string.
- To use:
  call MVFPA1 (see below)
  JSR $DDDD

Resulting string is returned starting at $0100 and ending with a $00 valued byte.

6. MVFPA1

- move floating point number to FPA1
- To use:
  Load Y-register with high byte of floating point start address
  Load A with low byte of floating point start address JSR $DBA2

7. MVFPA2

- move floating point number to FPA2.
- To use:
  Load Y with high byte of floating point start address
  Load A with low byte of floating point start address
  JSR $DA8C

The next 4 routines use arguments in the two floating point accumulators, so use MVFPA1 and MVFPA2 first.

8. Addition

- FPA1 — FPA1 + FPA2
- To use:
  JSR $D86A

9. Subtraction

- FPA1 — FPA2 − FPA1
- To use:
  JSR $D853

10. Division

- FPA1 — FPA2/FPA1
- To use:
  JSR $DB12

11. Multiplication

- FPA1 — FPA2 * FPA1
- To use:
  JSR $D853

The next 9 routines use the value in FPA1 as argument so use MVFPA1 first.

12. COS

- FPA1 — COS (FPA1)
- To use:
  JSR $E261

13. SIN

- FPA1 — SIN (FPA1)
- To use:
  JSR $E268

14. TAN

- FPA1 — TAN (FPA1)
- To use:
  JSR $E2B1

15. ATN

- FPA1 — ATN (FPA1)
- To use:
  JSR $E30B

16. ABS

- FPA1 — ABS (FPA1)
- To use:
  JSR $DC58

17. EXP

- FPA1 — EXP (FPA1)
- To use:
  JSR $DFED

18. INT

- FPA1 — INT (FPA1)
- To use:
  JSR $DCCC

19. SQR

- FPA1 — SQR (FPA1)
- To use:
  JSR $DF71

20. LOG

- FPA1 — LOG (FPA1)
- To use:
  JSR $D9EA

21. GETLN

- gets a line from the keyboard. A line is terminated with a RETURN keystroke. The line is stored in the BASIC input buffer.
- To use:
  JSR $C560

22. STROUT

- writes a character string to the screen.
- To use:
    Load Y with high byte of start address of string
    Load A with low byte of start address of string
    JSR $CB1E
- Note:
    The string must be terminated with a 0-valued byte.

INDEX